To Berny

Best wishes

Desmond

WATER UNDER THE BRIDGE

30 YEARS IN INDUSTRIAL MANAGEMENT

Water Under the Bridge

30 years in Industrial Management

by

Sir Desmond Pitcher

The Memoir Club

First published in 2003 by
The Memoir Club
Whitworth Hall
Spennymoor
County Durham

British Library Cataloguing in
Publication Data.
A catalogue record for this book
is available from the
British Library.

ISBN: 1 84104 048 7

Typeset by George Wishart & Associates, Whitley Bay.
Printed by Bookcraft (Bath) Ltd.

To Norma my wife, my daughters Stephanie and Samantha and my sons George and Andrew.

I would like to express my thanks to Mrs Doreen Holtermann for her help in producing the early scripts.

Contents

Illustrations

Foreword
by Rt Hon Michael Portillo MP

I FIRST MET Des Pitcher when I was a junior minister, and the government was considering him for a public appointment. I had already interviewed a succession of top business people whose reputations went before them, and each of them accordingly behaved with a certain haughtiness. As Des says of himself, he speaks quietly and carries an accent. This tendency to talk a little indistinctly, combined with his large spectacles, created a professional air that was confirmed by the pad of A4 lined paper resting on his lap. While I spoke he, somewhat disconcertingly, wrote. When it was his turn to talk, he referred to several pages of notes prepared beforehand. I had before me a thoughtful man who did not take his right to do the job for granted, and who left nothing to chance, or even hazards of memory.

This book confirms those first impressions. Throughout his business career, Des Pitcher took management seriously. A theme of this account of his life is his exasperation with those who could not appreciate the value of management techniques and experience, especially methodology that was based on proven practices.

Des is not from that generation that learnt its theories of management at business school. As a boy his mind related to physics and mathematics in a way that it could not to language, and as a young man he trained as an electrical engineer. Those must be the origins of his rigorous mental application to problem-solving; and he evinces a quiet certainty about his conclusions that you might think typical of a scientifically trained mind. Such self-confidence is not to everyone's taste.

Nor, clearly, were Pitcher's 'foreign ideas': management methods and disciplines picked up in the United States and elsewhere, which made perfect sense to him because they were rigorous and because he had seen them work. It is an irony that this Scouser, born within the sounds of the bells of St Nicholas's Church, Pier Head, Liverpool, should find himself so frustrated with the ways of his own country.

He expresses his deep disappointment that over the course of his career Britain's companies manufacturing aircraft, computers, cars, buses and trucks have passed under foreign ownership. He puts that down to failure by politicians to pursue a national industry strategy, using the purchasing power of government, to ensure the development of strong British companies in the most critical manufacturing industries. He laments that business people, civil servants and academics are not interchanged during their careers, and therefore lack a common national purpose. Politicians come out of this book badly, for their lack of vision, selfishness and short-termism. But actually the British business people as he describes them often lack the discipline that Des considers a key to success in America. In the UK – in business as well as in the government – meetings have to be arranged long in advance, and have to be minuted, yet the participants may not implement what is decided!

Des's private life has been an interesting one. His childhood, especially during World War II when he was evacuated, deprived him of much contact with his father, mother or sister. He was dismissed from the Boy Scouts for his rebellions against things he believed to be unfair. Two of his marriages have failed, though fortunately his third, to Norma, is a great success. The amateur psychologist might speculate as to how those events have contributed to the high values he places on loyalty. His harshest comments are reserved for those who have been underhand. Correspondingly, my experience of Des is that he attaches himself to friends with absolute loyalty.

Few things have been as distasteful for Des as when, having moved from Littlewoods to United Utilities for a lower salary, he was targeted as a 'fat cat' in the Labour Party's slur campaign against the private industries. Of course, as Des points out, the period since Labour came into government has been characterised not by lower pay for executives, but by higher pay for politicians!

The campaign against the 'fat cats' was highly effective because it appealed to a sadly characteristic British resentment against people who are successful, unless they are footballers or rock stars. For much of the population, profit is associated with greed and misconduct. In some ways, perceptions have got worse since Des left business to devote himself to his charities and his family.

Des Pitcher fears that a Britain that has lost so much productive capacity is muddling by. Our consumer boom cannot forever disguise our economic decline. As I have said, Des puts much of the blame on politicians. It won't be a surprise that I do not entirely agree, if only because I see no reason why British politicians should be any more unimaginative, selfish and short-termist than those in other countries.

I feel that Des gets nearer to identifying our national malaise when he points to a distinctive British culture within business and towards business. That mentality within business engendered much hostility towards Pitcher in a number of jobs he did; and that prejudice against success and profit fuelled the 'fat cats' campaign, which damaged our enterprise economy as much as it did the Tories.

I hope that, over time, champions may come forward to speak in favour of enterprise, and to explain that we depend on it to create wealth. All our dreams of greater social justice or better public services will come to nothing unless enterprise succeeds. Des Pitcher's honest book helps to explain that. In most countries his story – of how a boy from Liverpool, entirely without material advantages, rose to the top – would be a cause for celebration. Is Britain really so mean a place, so lacking in magnanimity, that we cannot take pleasure from Des Pitcher's remarkable achievements?

A Conclusion to Start

Personal Reflections

GEORGE PITCHER, who is no relation, but a PR guru, said I should write the Conclusion to this book at the beginning. I am not sure if this is a good idea or a bad one, but he said that most people don't read the Conclusion until they've read the rest of the book and tend to jump to the end of it. Whereas if the Conclusion comes first people can pick out the parts of the book they may want to study in more detail.

Aspiring to be judged against your fellows is a very hollow ambition and a very unsatisfying one at that. I believe that in my industrial career I played a significant role in five large enterprises over a thirty year period, every single one of which increased its performance when I took over responsibility, until I moved on to the next job. Some of the improvements were dramatic: Leyland Truck and Bus made almost £100 million profit; Plessey share price increased from 36p to 736p with profits rising proportionately; Littlewoods' valuation was 30 times up on completion of my Chief Executive role; and United Utilities profits were up year on year, shares up and down with the political mood of the moment. So when I look around at my peers I don't find many who have that kind of track record over that period of time.

It was largely because I saw myself as some sort of management fixer. I didn't want to be part of a management institution and work for ever for one company. That stemmed from my youth, I think. But whatever I took responsibility for, I wanted to leave it much better than I found it. I think that was a fact in all cases.

Then we move on to the question of style. This is where I have had my principal conflicts. My detractors would never admit it but that was

1

the basis of their objections to me. It was simply my style, which clashed with others, and I wonder if that applies to every other Chief Executive who decides to leave a position. It is not because his performance is poor but because his style is not compatible with that of the people he is working with. My style unquestionably was difficult for people to comprehend. I think the reason was that during the middle part of my life from late teens until my thirties I had the great privilege of being employed by the Sperry Rand Corporation, at one stage about that time America's third largest corporation. They took me from a technician to Managing Director. They transported me to many countries in the world. They took me through extensive training in computers and in management and they did for me what no education in Britain could possibly do: they provided me with first class comprehensive training and education in the field of Corporate Management.

My Rule Book – 10 Management Principles

1. Be open to colleagues (secrecy kills initiative).
2. Listen to yourself (the big falls come when you heed other advice than your intuition).
3. Keep eye and conversation contact with as many staff and customers as possible (each one has a message).
4. Don't take your personal life for granted (it is much more difficult to repair or heal than a dented car).
5. Walk the floor (sensing the business is the base for good decisions).
6. Travel widely (see how other parts of the world do it).
7. Widen your business/social experience (provides better framework for your own activities).
8. Don't have bankers on your board (their services are best used as providers).
9. Play your strong suit (every manager must be a professional something).
10. When the going is good look out for the rough (which will certainly be coming).

When I arrived back in England to work at Leyland Truck and Bus at the beginning of my forties people had difficulty understanding me in terms of my management approach, particularly its openness. Everything was on the table; no secrets in the company; there was inclusiveness in terms of spending time with the shop stewards and people on the shop floor. My peers seemed to disregard my prior knowledge because as they had not experienced it, they could not relate to it. Whether it came from what I did, why I spoke the way I did, they jumped to the conclusion that seemed to follow me through my life in British industry: that I was simply the lad from Liverpool, who had been nowhere, achieved nothing and had found himself by some stroke of luck in positions of high importance. They couldn't answer that question and that is the way they frequently treated me. They were missing the point that I was bringing with me international experience which was easy to apply to British industries. I didn't like it, but it didn't necessarily worry me and in the end I formed the view that it was an ideal form of protection.

I even met this mentality ten years after Truck and Bus in the early 1980s when I was at Littlewoods where I was employing extensive management techniques which people seemed to believe were unlikely to work because they had no foundation to their application. In particular I brought in the Five Year Plan. The whole purpose of a five-year plan is not to compute the numbers for the next five years in absolute detail, but to set down the aspirations of a particular Division so that you know what you are trying to achieve. When you get to Year 2 you may well have to change something, but not void the underlying commitment to the main financial tenets of growth, investment and profitability. You may decide to do it somewhat differently in the new Years 2, 3 and 4 and likewise in Year 3 for new Years 3, 4, 5 and 6. At the end of five years you will hopefully get what you were trying to achieve, even though you had varied the plan. It's rather like an aircraft landing: on a flight path moving up and down finally to land at the right point. This approach was bitterly resisted and one day one of the management team said to me, 'We are all wasting our time here. We have so many important things to do rather than fooling around with what is going on in the next five years.' My response was, 'If you had thought about these things five years ago you would not be here now. Unless you climb out of this mentality of going to work every day, doing something and then going home, and start thinking and working forward then you never are going to get out of the constant running mode you find yourself in.'

As I saw it this approach by other people was helpful because they put me to the test on some of my ideas. They rather took the view that they didn't know how to put me to the test. They seemed to take the view that my background and presumably my intelligence was very limited and treated me in that way. Of course they didn't get away with it, but that's another story. Consequently from time to time I made difficult decisions, but these are things that management have to do if they want to make the job work.

The third point, on reflection, is that you do have to have sufficient skill in depth to manage a large enterprise. You do not under any circumstances attempt to influence more than six or eight people under your direct control. Indirectly you may influence another thirty below them, but if you have the acceptance of thirty people as to what you want to do and where you want to go and an openness of com-munication on what is happening, how things can be improved and how sure you are you can get to the destination you are currently pursuing, then it works. You don't do this by yourself. It is all about other people doing things for you and of course more people doing things for them in their turn. I always think the best statement of what good management really is, is getting people to do things you want them to do because that's what they think they want to do. If you have to shout at people you will never get there.

Sometimes when you talk to people you realize that they have an idea which you have been trying to implant in their mind, but they are expressing it better than you did. If you can plant an embryonic thought in people's minds, they will put the meat on the bone and go and do the job. To do that you need a particular style and that can be simply to respect somebody's ideas, even when you don't know where they are coming from. I am not prone to shouting and making a fuss. I know many things have been said about me but I can never recall being involved in an outspoken shouting situation in my business career.

Everybody who wants to be a General Manager or Chief Executive must have a particular skill. It may be that he knows all about that particular business. If he's running a retail business he should be a very good retailer. Then everybody will admire that skill because that is his background. Of course it is best used if he moves around to different companies and gets experience and cross pollination of the processes and what is involved in the retail business, particularly in my case, as I never had an over-riding desire to stay with a company very long. My periods in jobs were consecutively 15, 5, 10 and 5 years. I think that five years by any standards is a reasonable time in a management role. Then you need to have something you can immediately apply, which in my case was systems. My origins in management training systems were a natural to me for some reason or another, possibly because my background was principally in maths and physics rather than English. The logic in systems and the integration of systems through the whole operation of a company can give you an insight or an observation as to how the company ought to be run.

Finally my reflections on the fourth key element of my business career: that is strategy. I always try to see the vision; always try to see what I could really do with this company to make it really good. This has to be done against the background that it has got to work economically as a company. Unless it is generating its own efficiency and its own wealth from outside to cover investment and borrowings, it is going to wither on the vine. So economic growth is the first objective, but the strategic objective is to find out what sort of company it is going to be in five years time or even longer, since it may well be that you recognize early on that the opportunities cannot be achieved by you alone. Five years is enough for any management role and then it is time for someone else to take over the reins.

This was the worst area of my corporate experience in Britain. It is better in America where it is a constant theme. People were always searching for the next product line, new markets and how to optimize investment, how cash flow would be recirculated and so on. We would sit for twenty or thirty days a year at different hotels around the world just discussing these matters. Many business ideas and opportunities came out of these meetings. For instance the VP for US Defence Systems had an excellent idea in terms of the German Air Traffic Control that we thought we had no hope of putting together. With my people and his experience we did get the German ATC contract, which was very rewarding.

It is frustrating to see how much damage has been done to vision. I am not sure we are too well served by non-Executive Board members, but if people are going to be non-Executives they should be totally contemporary business people, about the same age and not much older than the Executives. I realized when I got past sixty that I was becoming a burden to other people. I could see people around me who were seventy and hadn't the vaguest idea of the sort of picture they were creating with their comments. So vision is so important. It is hard to find a British company that has got that kind of vision, which has not been prone to influence from the media or from the chattering classes, who take it off the track of pursuing any foresight it might have. Of course that is a recipe for gross failure for the company.

Disregarding Sperry, which was the company that gave me so much, I most enjoyed being involved with the Plessey Company. Seventy per cent of its staff were graduates, a highly intelligent group of people pioneering some of the most advanced technology in the world and yet with a strong commercial bent. Peter Marshall, the Finance Director, and I were a very compatible couple. Sir John Clark, the Chairman, son of the founder, had a very enquiring mind. Sometimes he was criticized for that by smaller intellects, who made lofty comments about his ideas, but he was always exploring what could be done. He saw his job as being to stimulate people and help them.

I think my worst job was United Utilities. In retrospect I should not have taken that job. I didn't need it. I was reaching the age of fifty-eight, a good age for retirement. My vision for United Utilities was quite clear. It was to make it a major company in the utilities industry with a mass application of technology to bring it up to be a leading company in the world with an international market place – and we were getting there. In reality no-one else wanted that apart from the executives. The Government didn't particularly want it; they would rather have the company to slag off as a rip-off public utility. The employees certainly didn't want it because they wanted it to stay as it had always been. The press didn't want to hear about it. They never referred to our international achievements, never mentioned our investment programme and they were not interested in the massive development in the emerging technologies, the computer systems we put in during that period. It was the wrong place to go at that stage of my career. However, it was interesting and stimulating, and I suppose it is what led me to write this book. I believe there are some provocative comments, which may re-visit the past for, perhaps, helpful purposes. We shall see.

Finally my family life. I didn't really want to write about my family in this book, but a critic said it is empty and sounds as if I am hiding something if I omit it. I have been immensely pleased with my family: two lovely daughters, and two young sons who have yet to show what they want to do in their lives and careers. There is no hurry. They are still in their early twenties. Then I have had the good fortune to have a very affectionate and loving partner in my wife who, for the last fifteen years that we have been together, has done so much for me. If you are divorced twice you must begin to doubt your ability to create relationships. You tend to blame other people. Some of that is true, but you must face up to the fact that some of it must be your own fault simply for getting into the position in the first place. It does need a community of spirit between two people to really understand and help each other. That doesn't mean a namby pamby partner, who agrees with anything, but it does mean community of concern, community of inquisition, community of expectation and mutual needs. In some respects that has made the last fifteen years of my life the most enjoyable. I have seen my family grow up and have grandchildren. I have been able to enjoy my life in somewhat quiet contemplation, relaxing and watching what other people are now doing who are still active in business.

The Political and Social Environment

An English football manager who, although well acquainted with English football, has done very little in the international arena in recent years, made the comment that we really have a very vain attitude towards football. This arises from the fact that we constantly watch ourselves on television in the Premiership and other matches. We have the state of mind that somehow or other, because we see a lot of English football, it is the best in the world.

The plain fact of the matter is that England is a small country with limited, and even in some cases declining, skills and it is more likely it is way below the best. He continued by saying that once it is recognized who we are and where we are, then there is some possibility that we would move up and compete more effectively with other nations.

It seemed to me on hearing that remark and reading through my own recollections, that the statement had a far wider application than simply football. I have watched and even been part of the continuing decline of British industry *vis-à-vis* the competition from other countries. I have seen the demise of most major industries owned and run from this country. We have no truck manufacturing companies. We have no total aeroplane manufacture, only partial. Our computer industry is owned abroad. Our telecommunications industry is in part ownership. We have played little part in the space industry. Our coal and steel industries have virtually disappeared. One by one our utilities companies go into foreign ownership.

All these things have happened while other countries have continued to strengthen their position, not simply the US and Japan, but also a variety of South-East Asian countries and in particular in

Europe. Italy and France both have improved and strengthened their positions in the vital industries.

From my experience it is not who runs the country but how it is run that is the fundamental question to be answered properly if the declining industrial fortunes of this country are to be reversed.

Under both Governments I have seen at Leyland and at Sperry the chance for us, the British, to be one of the two major truck manufacturers in Europe blown away, and the prospect for us to be the real driving force in information technology through the ICL/Sperry merger to be ignored, for very largely chauvinistic reasons, or quite possibly in some cases because personal ambitions were being interfered with.

The plain fact of the matter is that no Government of any political persuasion has ever shown a clear, appropriate, international, trading strategy, which is a fundamental reason for the decline of British industry.

Dealing with the British Government is too complicated. No Government has either the imagination or the interest to understand how they set the framework for the development of industry in Britain. As a consequence the businesses have become part of a market and are traded as market entities by the finance institutions, who really are the only major means of support for British companies.

It really goes further than this in that the ability of the British companies to obtain working capital, because of the inter-relationships between the banks and the Government, is very limited. Consequently they very seldom have sufficient working capital for long enough to make progressive improvements in productivity and overseas market penetration in the way that they should be.

It must look anyway as if the influence of Government is declining. The agenda seems to be set by growing numbers of single issue groups who, through a willing media, press their special interest and self interest cases, resulting in knee-jerk Government responses out of context with the issues they are dealing with. Consequently constant change and destabilization takes place, ever undermining the sound financial, economic and social base that the country must have to progress.

The one country which of course is the exception to this is the USA. Its market is of such a size and such scope that it can, through the discrete placement by the US Government of major contracts, carry out a co-ordinated, well-planned, rational, industrial and economic development programme.

The message to me is clear – that the adversarial role of politics in relationships with industry, or even for that matter with the social groups, are now so disparate that there is a proper need to re-examine the way the country should be run, as opposed to how it is run. If any Government is to ever do this country any real service it will address that issue promptly and effectively.

One message that comes out of my comparisons is that unquestionably the fact that Britain operates in many separate constituent parts is not helpful. The relationships between business and university for instance are only commercial at the fringes, never in depth. The relationship between industry and the civil service is also extremely formal. There is no possibility at all, as there is in other countries, of senior professors and senior civil servants and senior industrialists changing jobs for a period of time, and bringing the community of spirit and purpose to the fore as a consequence of their broadened experience.

In particular there is very little transportability of any of the three groups outside the country. The businesses tend to be managed by people with very limited international experience. This is wholly inappropriate in the global competitive situation in which we find ourselves.

It also is an attitude of mind that what is right for the British market is right for all other markets. That is totally wrong of course. The gross national product per head is a direct influence on whether the specification for a product should be higher or lower than the British. In an analysis of the low income countries, low specs and appropriate specs have to be drawn, not simply taking British specs and modifying them in a minor sort of way.

There is too, in the approach to these markets, a need for co-ordination with the Government, particularly in terms of any aid possibilities. It is too spotty; it should be concentrated. It should be handled on a project basis, as the French situation, not on the beggar's bowl principle that currently applies to industrial activities seeking to sell outside this country.

But coming back to the failure, or the immobility, of people between the constituent groups of education, industry and Government, to name but three; there is also the situation *vis-à-vis* the education of Britain. It never has been, and seemingly nobody wants to slant it towards, a more technically oriented type of education. In a world where technology has changed in most countries, and the standards of life and nature of social behaviour, we still shy away from the subjects of physics and mathematics which should be key and prime to the development of our youth.

It shows itself in that most emphasis on education is in the education of the unemployed, when in reality that may be totally inappropriate education for any possible employment they may subsequently find. The division between education and people in work is totally wrong.

The whole education process should accelerate when people find themselves in jobs, and constant effort should be made to improve their level of knowledge and ability in their jobs by workplace training right throughout the whole organization, and for that matter, right through-out one's individual career.

This is formally done in other countries and therefore is engendered in our competitors' workforce. The emergence of the tiger economy in the countries of South-East Asia is all about their ability to adopt new technologies and transport manufacturing techniques across the world very quickly, and very cheaply. The emphasis on technical studies in higher education has developed their intellect and vigour and led them to apply technology in their own country.

The Government's approach to education is vital, if we are to improve our economic and industrial performance: more science as opposed to arts, media and social studies.

On a personal scale I can see that from wherever you start the opportunities for personal progression are there if you are determined enough to seek them out and pursue them vigorously. It is unquestionably a major help if you have had, particularly in your early career, considerable international experience and therefore you can bring direct comparisons between German and American methods of doing things and the manner in Britain.

I suppose this is best exemplified by comparing American meetings to British ones. Americans meet at short notice, informally, without agenda or minutes. Then they all go away and carry out the agreed decisions without follow up or further questions. In Britain a meeting has to be organized considerably ahead of time. There has to be an agenda, papers and minutes, which nobody ever really reads, and then quite frequently the decisions that have been made are only in part executed after the end of the meeting.

This question of individual communication and openness and a desire to communicate has got to be addressed. We all need to act in conformity, as other countries do, to maximise opportunities and utilise all the constituent parts of Britain to make a strong economic and commercial country.

Lastly we cannot ignore the position of the media. Profit is not something which a few people live in splendour off or in the pursuit of which people exploit the masses for their own selfish ends. Profit is in reality the driving force behind investment and economic growth and the main provider of pensions, insurance and savings for the community at large. If profits fall so, dramatically, do industrial growth and social welfare. Profit is positive cash flow, life and growth; losses are negative cash flow and death.

Reading back my experiences, it really is to me a depressing picture of economic and social decline partly compensated, if that is possible, by a substantial growth of consumerism and all other associated stimuli that are used for implicating and even disguising from the general public the underlying decline of the wealth of our country. It seems doubtful if our consumerism approach is to continue: leastways everything we have invested will be depreciated to so low a value that it will be incapable of sustaining sufficient economic activity to properly support this generation or generations to come.

The American Challenge, in the sixties, struck a chord with the French. Unless they could respond to American industrial dominance through technology, their country would be in the same condition that we are in today. This actually stimulated the French into a substantial working programme to develop, support and push its major industries with great success. We today unquestionably need this same definition of our position and need to set our goals for economic and industrial growth in a programme which all the constituent parts of the country can in some measure support, if we are to repeat what the French did to transform themselves from a failing industrial nation to one with a massive capability in most key industrial areas.

Politics and Business

So now I will go into some specific instances of my activities, which involve politicians and business. The first that I got dramatically involved in was in the late sixties, early seventies when Sperry was interested in merging its Univac division, which was then the world's second largest computer company in large main frames with ICL, Britain's biggest computer company. ICL would get the controlling share interest. Univac would make the key appointments on the Board, particularly in the area of finance. This would have made ICL, overnight, three or four times its previous size, taking on board very large customer bases, particularly in Germany, France, Italy and Spain as well as the UK. As you will read later we had endless discussions with the Government over this. As today, even in the early seventies the Government was trying to be European and a compliant decision emerged to suit the Brussels view. The result, the early demise of the continental computer. The same fate came later for the British company and worst of all an opportunity was lost in Britain to create a substantial enduring base to build a major information technology company in the United Kingdom.

My second major experience was being the Managing Director of Leyland's Truck and Bus Division and discussions that we held to try and merge with Fiat Trucks giving Leyland the controlling interest and basing the headquarters in England. Clearly any merger or partnership of that arrangement was fraught with all sorts of problems. Indeed the Pirelli Dunlop merger at about that time had suffered major difficulties but the Leyland/Fiat merger would have produced a large established truck and bus industry which covered the length and breadth of Europe and had some chance of being a serious competitor. In fact it would have been a real competitor against Mercedes, who were then market leaders.

The lost opportunity to consolidate Leyland Truck and Bus with Fiat Trucks removed any prospect of a UK truck company securing a long term substantial market share in UK and continental Europe. Grow or die: another opportunity lost meant the demise of the British truck industry.

Plessey was Britain's largest telecommunications company. I was Managing Director of the Telecommunications Group which was most of the company. After many political battles which you'll read in the relevant chapter, you will see that they finally secured control of both the development and the manufacture of System X, a very satisfying thing indeed. Thus they became a major contractor in the modernization of Britain's telecommunications network, putting Britain ahead with a national digital network. This was an example of political involvement in the way that politics should be involved, creating a market situation and seeing how best contractors and suppliers could meet it. Not restructuring the company or lending the company money, but quite simply using market clout to make it work to the best effect for them as Government customers and other customers as well.

The experience of my ten years of running Littlewoods was a diverse and interesting situation. There was Government involvement in that one. People may find it strange that the Government played a major role in Littlewoods, but they did. Littlewoods was a mail order, chain stores, property, finance and Football Pools organization. The Pools business was a monopoly of long odds–short stake gambling. For a long time some members of the Government had wanted it to be replaced by a national lottery. Littlewoods mounted a massive campaign, obviously out of self-interest, to stop this happening. It argued on a high moral ground, that gambling was bad for people, particularly the addictive kind of gambling that was easy to adhere to like a national lottery, scratch cards, and that kind of thing. We stressed particularly the work we had done, taking a very low profit out of Littlewoods. We had built up a Trust, the Football Trust to be used for re-building stadiums after events such as the Hillsborough disaster, and to fund sports and arts – to help Britain's rather poor sports facilities. It also gave the arts a boost to bring their level up to the American and European standards. So we had the Sports and Arts Foundation and the Football Trust.

The way the Lottery was operated lost the embedded loyalty the Football Pools held owing to its different marketing approach. The concept of Football Pools was marketed in such a way that you had an embedded capture of your customer base which hardly ever fell, year in and year out, whereas a lottery is a fickle thing. It has no intellectual value and consequently people get tired of numbers and it declines very quickly. There were two prime arguments that we conveyed to the Government. One was that a lottery is not a self-sustaining activity. It's a medium-term activity and it is generally raising money for one particular purpose. The second point we raised which we were adamant about, and indeed I hoped they would take on board but in fact they didn't, was the structure of the trusts. Trusts of that nature must be totally independent of any outside interference and must be very, very visible as to how they perform. Otherwise they quickly give the product itself a tarnished image and people move away from it on the grounds that not only are they not getting any winnings, but the Government is using the money for wasted causes. There can be nothing more spectacular than what happened with the Lottery in Britain in the last four years, the much rehearsed Wembley Stadium, and the Dome, the Government talking as though they owned all that money and running the Lottery as if the funds raised were hypothecated taxes for the Ministry of Culture. This was all done in a way that completely undermined any chance that the public would have any long-term faith in the activity.

And finally my 5-year stint at United Utilities during which North West Water became a utility operator of all the important utilities. It had the huge investment task of improving the quality and health of the water and an even more massive civil engineering operation which nobody ever saw or took much interest in. Why should they? No one wants to think about the removal of the tons and tons of waste which we humans produce in one form or another in our everyday lives. We had an ambitious overseas programme. This was quite a spectacular success in so many countries, which would have grown had it been sustained and maintained and pursued in order to compete on a serious level with the French, who were growing increasingly concerned about the competition that we were mounting against them. This was probably the best example of how inadequate politicians pursuing any line of argument pretend to be acting in the public interest, when they are damaging a major growth industry.

The revitalised Utilities could have been a major new international industry operating in developed countries and tackling some of the poverty in the poorer countries by ensuring the provision of water, sewerage and electricity. A lack of understanding in Government and a greed for taxes ensured it did not.

When I began my career thirty years ago there was a variety of British made cars; today all volume car manufacturers are foreign owned.

There were a number of world-famous airframe manufacturing companies making state-of-the-art commercial aircraft, e.g. the British Aircraft Corporation BAC 1-11, the Vickers VC-10 and the De Haviland Trident which in its time was the fastest commercial aircraft in the world. Today, whilst we make components assembled into airframes abroad, we neither make nor own a Commercial Airframe Company.

There was a proliferation of fledgling computer manufacturers who over the last thirty years have been consolidated into ICL which in its turn is now a Japanese company.

Numerous truck manufacturers, Leyland, AEC, Guy, to name but a few, have suffered consolidation or closure and then foreign takeover.

This loss of control of major sections of British industry and its subsequent effect on the security and wealth of the nation arose by direct or indirect Government interference and a series of mergers without the benefit of a national strategy.

The mergers were opportunist deals for in many cases the companies were incompatible not only in products but also in markets. The thin rationale was that big is beautiful but the organisation task was beyond the ability of the new management and for that matter any management.

The Department of Trade and Industry is a small but vital depart-ment. Unlike the big spending departments its prime task is facilitating the creation of wealth and value to ensure the country has the resources to fund the spending programmes of the larger, departments.

At the time of writing this section the Secretary of State for trade is Ms Patricia Hewitt who seems to be pursuing a feminist agenda of employment conditions for women which could be handled by other Government departments. These are very worthy causes yet there seems little by the way of a national strategy for industry emerging from the department. Such strategies in France and some Far East countries have resulted in a sounder more broad-based industrial structure, giving more durable long growth.

Conservative Governments don't enthuse about plans but you might expect this Labour Government to relish the prospect of creating such a National Strategic Industrial Plan.

We have seen in recent years an ever-increasing growth in the number of regulations affecting business, which consume management time and ability, cash and other resources.

The question of a national industrial strategy needs urgent addressing. I mention elsewhere the profound effect the Government purchasing policy can have; but there are two issues that need consideration to reverse the wealth erosion phenomenon.

Corporate governance and company mergers
Trading in companies must take into account the consideration of short- and long-term social effects on shareholders, employees and customers. The company must fully address the concerns of these groups. The final decision must rest with the shareholders, but they must be much better informed.

If this had been a mandatory requirement thirty years ago the industrial scene would be very different today.

The second salient strategic issue is the reputation of profit which has for some time been seen in the eyes of the public as a rip-off.

Profit arose as a Victorian concept basically to satisfy bankers of the trading prospects of a company. Profit is the main driver of investment. Its true value and reputation diminish daily as a consequence of what seem to be major scandals or accounting errors perpetrated by major companies, in Britain certainly, but principally in the United States.

Politicians are pursuing the usual response to this public discontent by encouraging committees to come out with recommendations regarding the roles and functions of company boards. The appointment of yet more ciphers to attend the board meeting will make no difference. Running a business is full time job and best use must made of vital management time.

To eliminate accounting failures and restore public confidence a new radical transparent disclosure procedure is vital. Transparency can only be achieved by clearer and simpler accounting statements. Companies have made profits and still gone broke. Companies that have cash and pay their bills remain solvent even though they may not look exciting traders.

Company accounts should be stated as cash accounts. There should be a clear distinction between the cash invested, the cash arising from depreciation and, most importantly, the cash generated from the ongoing business.

They should be supported by a total cash certified statement. There will be some surprises; many companies look profitable with negative cash flows, but there is clearly a limit to how long that situation can continue.

Cash accounts specifically highlighting positive cash generation or a negative cash outflow would tell the story very quickly. Any subsidiary, regardless of the ownership to which the parent company gives or takes cash, must be fully consolidated in the parent company's cash statement.

The time has come for a truly realistic reliable reporting process; nothing else will cure the problem. This Government claims to be a modernizing Government; now must be the time to make the changes in reporting and corporate takeover.

PREFACE

The Experience

I BELIEVE IT MIGHT BE helpful to explain the reason why I put pen to paper to describe my business career. The first reason soon spawned others, so in reality there are three motives for writing this book. A close friend of mine, a little older, had followed a similar career. By not retiring at a sensible age he was beginning (through his mannerisms) to show stress and difficulties, particularly at dinner and social occasions. Tragically, one day, quite suddenly and without warning, he committed suicide. After the initial grief, his family were concerned that he'd actually done so much and experienced so many things and yet so little was known about him, his work and achievements, and they recommended to me that I should, if I could, put down as much as I could remember of my journey through industry. That has not been a very easy task. As I look back I realize that I've been alive over 20,000 days. You begin to accept that your memory is not as good as it was in your youth. You also begin to wonder how to separate the personal from the business activities and even what points are, even to yourself, more significant than others.

The second reason I put forward is that from time to time at schools and universities I have given lectures to graduates on the experience of being in management. I found this very stimulating and they seemed to find it interesting, if only because they had often had lectures from barristers and accountants and the members of the more stereotyped professions. I seemed to be the first person to put the idea of industrial management into their young minds and make the argument that a career in industry could be an interesting and rewarding vocation. They had before them the choice of established professions: the Forces; Law; Finance, so I hope in some small way I helped some of them form the

21

view that whilst a career in industry is a long process it also is a very rewarding experience.

Lastly, reflecting on my partial draft, I wondered if there were any messages to give. There is really one quite clear one: that is that for one reason or other I have spent most of my industrial career concerned with international activities and having to influence or work with politicians. I have most certainly been affected by political decisions. It made me wonder why it is that most of British industry now belongs to foreign companies.

Why is this? Why do our manufacturing industries get progressively taken over by foreign companies with the loss of control by and the loss of commitment to our country? It seems to me that firstly we have the frequently criticized short term mentality of institutional investors, managed, by and large, by people who have never worked in industry, few of whom have any international experience.

There is the penchant for Governments of whatever inclination to want to interfere directly with the workings of companies and there are examples in my book of Government managing the outcome in a way that they think is appropriate for their political ends.

The involvement hasn't all been negative. Some has been quite helpful, as you can see from the System X experience in telecommunications. It is quite right and proper that the Government should play a pivotal role in the future of commerce and industry in the country. After all, that is, in the end, the foundation for future prosperity for the coming generations. But consider its attempt to influence current management and regulate or intervene in everyday business activities. Is that the right thing to do? Indeed some of the strategic issues in my book indicate how great opportunities have been lost by just that kind of political intervention. The French in the 1960s became aware of the dangers of technological domination, in particular from the US, the American challenge as it was termed then, and their Government set about facilitating over the long term the regeneration of their computer and technological industries and the creation of their aerospace industries, which are now larger than that of the Americans.

The French Government of the day laid down their strategic plan, a long term plan, and facilitated the achievement of the programme by pressure or by assistance. That clearly must be right.

The most effective way for governments to influence companies, once they have an industrial strategy, is by using their clout as customers by placing orders and volumes in such a way to have their strategic thinking materialize. This approach the American and French Governments used extensively to major effect. The last British Government used the policy on limited occasions, for example with System X, described later in the book. The present Government, being obsessed with social issues and political consequences, even if it understands the problem would be unlikely to follow that purely because it would be contrary to its political nature to see industry as anything other than a job and tax provider. It dislikes the disruptive effect of industrial change, while jumping at every opportunity to try and save a failing business.

Governments need an intellectual ability to define an industrial strategy and the wisdom to avoid interference. That is the main thrust of the words that follow, save the inevitable question: 'On looking back, was it worth it?' There are particular downsides to being in high profile public industrial positions. The media is clearly one. You are therefore, after politicians, a large target for media comment. As I say elsewhere in the book I took this as part of the job. The other downside is that you have, like most industrialists, a restricted personal life. We are not able to spend time with our families. We miss out on the experience of our children growing up. We experience frequently one divorce and sometimes two or even more as a consequence of not being able to establish relationships with our families because we simply do not have the time. In my case I believe I was very lucky. My third relationship and marriage has been one which has been as close and meaningful and supportive as words can possibly describe. I am particularly lucky in that whilst having four children from two marriages I have been able to maintain close loving relationships with all of them. To a large extent the ability to maintain and develop these relationships was down to my children themselves. Like most young people they have a high degree of tolerance and a lot of optimism. That very much acted in my favour in maintaining contact with them. It is strange but true that intolerance and cynicism tend to show later in adult life. Not all executives were as lucky as me, particularly if their careers finished in a crash prematurely, as so often can be the case.

But the upside, people will say, is that you are well paid. Well, yes, you are, but for a great part of my working life taxation was high at 83 per cent and divorces are expensive, so I probably would have been better off working for myself, but of course less well off working in the bowels of the organization.

The principal benefit and enjoyment of a job like an executive's is the experience you get from extensive international travel, visiting different countries, and my time working and visiting the USA has been a particular pleasure. I have to say after my homeland it is my favourite country. The relatively smooth operation of capitalism through extensive competition resulting in such a high standard of living and health for the great majority of the population makes it a country which it is a joy to be in. I also enjoyed the many visits to South East Asia, and to those underprivileged countries which in recent years have shown so much enterprise in the development of their economies and their societies in the inscrutable oriental way that I don't think Western people really fully understand, in the same way that Orientals always question the methods and thinking of us Occidentals. At home or abroad, there were many meetings and dinners and experiences, most of which were pleasant and enjoyable, few of which were difficult. So my answer to the question did I enjoy it is 'Yes'. I did not live to work, I worked to live. Not simply in the pecuniary sense but also because of the many experiences I was fortunate enough to enjoy in the senior positions that I had the honour to occupy over that thirty year period. Of course, much of it was luck. From my beginnings in Liverpool I knew there had to be something better. My real break came when I went to Switzerland in 1960 and 1961. I realized it was a big wide world full of interesting opportunities if I wished to take them up. Yes – it was worth it. It was an exciting career. It was a rewarding career, if for nothing else than because every day was very, very different. And each day brought its challenges, its stimulation, and its setbacks. In the end, looking back over 20,000 days I doubt if I would have chosen any other route.

CHAPTER 1

Childhood

I WAS BORN ON 23 March 1935 at Smithdown Road Hospital, an old hospital, previously a workhouse, which was subsequently renamed Sefton General. It is a miserable establishment bordering on to a massive cemetery and on the odd occasion I have been back there I have formed the view it is not the sort of place you would normally choose to be born in.

One immediate benefit of being born in Smithdown Road was that you were entitled to become a so-called Dickie Sam. This is a title for a Liverpudlian born within sound of the bells of St. Nicholas's Parish Church at the Pier Head. Given a strong westerly on 23 March it would have been possible to hear the bells of St. Nicholas's. My friends joke that the first thing I did was to ask for a telephone.

About the only good thing I know about Smithdown Road Hospital was that Sir John Smith, of whom I would be a close friend in later years, was also born there, but slightly earlier than myself. John Smith, whilst a brewer by origin, subsequently became quite possibly the most successful Chairman of Liverpool Football Club, in particular during its great post-war period. I guess the first thing Sir John would have asked for at birth would have been a football.

The war started four years later in 1939. I was not terribly conscious of the fact that the war had started, but it certainly had a big effect on my early life. My father, whom I saw very infrequently, had really taken up a separate existence from my mother and was living in London working in a variety of management positions involved in the production of films. He was never really very successful although from time to time he was involved with some of the more memorable films, in particular *Genevieve* and *Heroes of Telemark*.

27

This meant that my mother effectively lived by herself in the Knotty Ash district. There is a place called Knotty Ash; it wasn't simply invented by Ken Dodd! Here my eldest sister joined the Women's Auxiliary Service, and my elder brother joined the Merchant Navy at the age of sixteen. I was hardly to know either of them until the 'teens of my life.

My second sister who was three years older than me presumably lived with my mother, although again I wasn't aware of any real contact with her until the age of seven or eight.

Looking back, I believe one of my feelings during this period was that everybody I knew seemed to disappear out of my life and in an odd sort of way I felt somewhat responsible for the war itself. My reaction to that was that there wasn't much I could do about it and it certainly wasn't my fault so I'd best forget about it. This experience may well have boded well for me in later years, when it wasn't unusual for people to try to make me feel responsible for things for which I was not, or even accuse me of things I wasn't associated with. When this happened I always had the same reaction as the one in my youth: it was nothing to do with me; there was nothing I could do about it, so there was no point worrying.

I, for reasons that were never really explained, spent a great deal of my time with my grandmother. I suspect that my mother, who like all women of her age at that time in the war was forced to take a job, probably found it better for me to be looked after by someone else in the family.

We lived in Opie Street, which is on Everton hill overlooking the Mersey. It wasn't a comfortable existence. There was an open fire which heated the adjacent iron stove, gas lights which were quite insignificant and miserable once it went dark, and an outside toilet which when I was five or so was a very unwelcome experience, particularly during the winter months.

Opie Street no longer exists. It was obliterated by the construction of horrendous high-rise towers which became buildings of squalor, loneliness and crime. The towers were subsequently knocked down

A small boy in Liverpool, 1939.

and replaced by inadequate modern council houses, masquerading as a form of new urban village development but lacking any real character. Opie Street in my childhood was a bright, lively place where the sun always shone, and there were always exciting new opportunities and experiences. Everton is one of the inner city areas from which the football team takes its name of which I was later to be a Director, sometime Deputy Chairman, over a period of ten years.

This was probably my first experience of kicking a ball. The preoccupation of the children in that area was, almost entirely, kicking a ball against gable end walls which had football posts chalked on them. The street, like rows of other streets to its left and right, was very steep, dropping down a hill to two major roads in the city, Great Homer

Street and Scotland Road. The vantage viewing point from the street was nothing short of magnificent. The whole vista of the river, the Wirral opposite and the Welsh hills could be seen from that one spot in the midst of a great urban conurbation. Going down to the main roads you could see the great mass of people going about their work in that wartime period. Particularly clear in my mind are the steam engines, the horses and people with handcarts, all then the predominant forms of transport, lorries being infrequently seen.

Close to Scotland Road was the overhead railway line that ran the seven miles of the dock system. The most interesting experience for a day out was to see the full extent of the dockland activity during the war. Occasionally you would get a trip to Southport because the overhead railway would connect with the Southport line. Most food was sold from handcarts in Great Homer Street and a special trip was always made on Saturday night to get the cheap but good cuts from the butchers' shops before they closed. It seemed at the time an ideal wonderland for a young boy, particularly one with a sense of curiosity who disliked being dragged round in his grandmother's hand and was keen to get out and explore this vibrant world around him.

Also living with us was my Uncle Albert, my mother's youngest brother. Albert acted very much like a father to me. He would buy me Boy Scout belts, and gave me a brand new penny every week. He would occasionally play games with me and was really a very likable all-round person, always full of fun, who had many friends visit the house with him.

So whatever the hardships of war and the inconvenience of the house, I think it was, in spite of the absence of my mother, a happy and interesting period of my life.

Albert would do some quite ridiculous things; it was his nature. One day he appeared at home with an incendiary bomb. The Germans were dropping thousands and thousands of incendiary bombs every night all around us. He placed this one on the mantelpiece over the fire. My grandmother asked him what did he think he was doing, in that stern way that grandmothers have to sons or grandsons of their establishment. He remarked that he had found it and brought it home as a souvenir. It was quite clear by the manner of my grandmother's response that he had to take it back to where it came from. His reply was: 'Do you want me to take it back to the Dock Road or do you want me to take it back to Germany?' That was a typical Uncle Albert remark.

An intriguing form of transport at the time was the Liverpool tram system. The trams were painted green and came in different vintages from those with open ends to much more modern ones, and perhaps later on the so-called Green Goddesses. There were many routes, crossing the centre of the city like a spider's web. I was frequently on the trams with or without my mother, visiting her or returning to Opie Street or going into town. The tramway was probably the most exciting part of my life at that stage, although the Blitz itself, seen by a small boy as a sort of grand firework display, left indelible memories on my mind, particularly after the May Blitz of 1941. Uncle Albert took me into town to see the blazing city when a large number of Liverpool's quite grand buildings were destroyed in that week-long blitz intended to close down the port, which had become the major European port connecting with America.

As a consequence of the war I didn't receive any early education nor even start school at the normal age as was the case with all of my contemporaries living in major cities during that period. After the bombing was finished, or the Germans decided it wasn't having any effect, the authorities thought it would be a good idea to evacuate all the children under a certain age from Liverpool. What the age was I am not quite sure, but I suspect it was seven. I recollect this period very clearly as this was the first time I had really had any effective contact with my sister Pamela.

One day we were peremptorily dumped, with a small suitcase, on a train at Birkenhead Woodside, with lots of other similar children, and said goodbye to our mother, with not the vaguest idea of where we were going or what was going to happen to us. Strangely enough we felt more excitement and promise with the train than fear at being separated from our parents; it was a typical Liverpool boys' and girls' day out, looking forward to new pastures and fresh experiences and a certain escape from the harshness of inner city life. We arrived at Ruabon to be separated into different groups going different ways.

Then another train arrived and took us on to Llangollen. It was a wet coldish day when we arrived there. A pretty town, particularly at the railway station which overlooks the River Dee which is wide enough and fast enough, with a pretty bridge to impress any visitor however young on arrival.

We were taken to the church hall and after a certain amount of processing, including being issued with a brown box containing a gas mask, we were handed out to various waiting people. In my case it was to two people, retired ladies who were sisters. Perhaps they were living on some inheritance in their quite modest establishment on Abbey Road which leads inevitably to Llangollen Abbey. They were very nice ladies, very kind and considerate to me, and it was helpful that my sister was lodged, boarded, whatever an evacuee did, at the next door but one house.

It wasn't an arrangement that lasted for very long because she never stopped crying and hated the whole situation, so that very shortly after arriving at Llangollen she was removed and evacuated to Blackpool. Nobody ever seemed to consult me about anything in those days; I just happened to watch things happen around me.

In some respects I preferred the hustle and bustle of the bombing of Liverpool and the trams and activities and certainly missed Uncle Albert, but adjusting to my lot as I tend to do. I quietly went through that two year period.

The ladies did their best to make me feel happy although they had no experience of small boys. They were devout church goers and I tagged along with them, sometimes three times on a Sunday, maybe because the other boarder there was the vicar at the church. Routine was pretty strict and standard, the harshest part I suppose being never allowed to play games on a Sunday but simply read books, preferably the Bible.

The house bordered on to the end of the Shropshire Union Canal. I would go out through the back hedge and take a walk up and down the canal, watching the fishermen and the weir at the end of the Llangollen Chain Bridge Hotel. The other interesting occupation was to walk down to the station to see the trains come and go. There weren't many on the way to Corbin from Ruabon and back but the odd steam train, which of course they all were, was an interesting sight to see.

The bit I didn't like about this period of my life was my first experience of school. This was partly conducted in the cinema, and on other occasions in the infants' primary school itself. Furthermore it was also quite frequently conducted in Welsh and having hardly got any grasp of English yet, it clearly wasn't much use to me to attempt to learn Welsh.

It was at school, I think, that I mostly felt that we weren't wanted. Clearly the other schoolchildren there, who were Welsh, didn't want us and obviously their parents didn't want us either. While they came to collect their own children, we were always left to our own devices to get to and from our temporary homes. There was a certain amount of resentment towards us from the Welsh. It is probably somewhat unfair but I think it largely emanates from the way they collectively treated me and others as a small children away from home during the war. They quite simply didn't want us; this I could feel and tell and experience. Perhaps I should have been evacuated to South Wales, where I have good friends and which I enjoy visiting.

The elderly ladies, however (if they were indeed elderly, and they could well have been middle-aged or even younger), were very kind and involved me in routine tasks of stamping cheques and explained to me in their own words what their life was all about. Years later I went back to see them. One had died and one was certainly then very elderly. Occasionally I now pass the house and wonder who lives there now. I certainly was indebted to Llangollen as climbing the hill to the castle and fording the river, watching the seasons come and go, introduced me to quite a different world I now know is called called 'the country'.

It probably was the very first change of activity in my very varied life that made me feel that there were other things to do apart from being where I was and doing what I did. Moving from the centre of a city to a lovely country village was an enjoyable experience and, as I say, I have a gratitude to those dear old ladies who did their best as surrogate mothers in very difficult circumstances.

I moved back, I guess about the age of eight or nine, to Knotty Ash, in Crofton Crescent, which was my parents' home. It was a house built by Liverpool Corporation in the thirties, a neat and tidy estate very close to where two main Liverpool roads cross, Queens Drive and Prescot Road. My mother had moved there in the early thirties when the roads weren't built, and stayed there all told some fifty-three years, so it really was in many respects the most permanent establishment ever in my life. The neighbours of course, like most people in those days, were good, decent and honest people and standards were high, discipline was strong.

At about this time, at the age of twelve, I found myself suffering, particularly in the right foot, from severe pains approximately every three or four weeks. These pains were of such severity that they restricted my walking and additionally restricted any recreational activities. This was diagnosed as gout, which made me a bit of a laughingstock amongst the boys. Gout is a very painful experience. Anyone who has had it, or who is in the medical profession, will tell you it's very severe. That in itself was bad enough, but it limited my scope for playing in team games and cut off my opportunity to play football which I particularly enjoyed: not all the time but sufficiently to limit my permanent inclusion in the school team. It didn't actually cut out cricket because of the shorter season and anyway you can drop out of a cricket team with less effect than you can in football. The gout stayed with me for many years until for some other reason I was in hospital and the doctor confirmed the complaint and put me on a relatively simple medicine that virtually cured it, or at least controlled it. If only that medicine had been available when I was twelve years old I am sure I would have enjoyed some years of playing football.

I was of course reunited with my sister and we became quite close friends during the growing years. Initially I went to an Infants School for a year or two in Old Swan which made me realize how inadequate my disjointed education in Wales had been. It had taught me very little, with very little sport. There was no 11+ examination, as there was nothing to be tested on, and I moved over to Highfield Secondary Modern School.

Highfield was a typical mixed school of its day, with girls at one end and boys at the other. If they spoke at all it was on the way to or from school. It was a school of harsh, if not overtly cruel, discipline; in other words they conducted a reign of terror. The teachers were mostly returned service people who had been reinstated after the war. I hated the place, so much so that my consciousness of my poor level of education started to show itself physically. I developed a very severe speech defect. This speech defect showed itself as an inability to sound 's' or 't' and led to a jumble of words which led to poor spelling and English for many years to come. I think it was the sheer dislike of the establishment that led me to sit for what was then called the 13+ examination, which had been introduced because of the recognition that many schoolchildren had had their education damaged because of the war.

I was one of the ten lucky boys, that's how I saw it at the time, to pass the 13+ examination and then went to the Old Swan Technical Institute. The Technical Institute was a revelation. The subjects of course were mathematics, physics, chemistry, some English and practical engineering with a strong technical bent. All these subjects I found easy to understand, and consequently enjoyed and I suddenly discovered that there was pleasure in learning. The older teachers, who had been there right through the war, were more mature and therefore more helpful and encouraging.

Consequently I thrived at this school, quite simply because I found I really did enjoy the learning process. I suppose it can be described as the foundation of my academic interests which grew as the years continued. These people showed close emotional support for my career and work. Few people understood me well as I became pretty good at covering up my inner views and feelings. This really arose I guess because the first ten or twelve years of my life were mostly spent by myself using my own resources to stimulate my interest but being subject to frequent change instigated by external forces.

Harking back to those times there were a number of moments which I vividly remember, particularly in May 1945 when I was playing in the garden by myself and hearing on the news that the European war was over. It gave me great pleasure to take this news to my mother who was spending some time with her friends in the local pub. They weren't quite sure whether to believe me at the time – a ten year old dashing in and telling them all the war was over – but certainly it became a night for outstanding celebration.

My main pursuit, and one that I conducted by myself, was engine spotting. I collected the various books of steam engine numbers and would spend many hours at Lime Street at the Edge Hill locomotive depot as far afield as Warrington until very late at night, which led to some consternation from my mother. Nevertheless she seemed to feel and understand that even at that age I was quite self-sufficient and was able to look after myself.

There was however a need also to be part of a social situation. That was a natural thing in Liverpool, where people have to belong to groups and organizations otherwise they are ostracized for being anti-social quite simply because they are just not considered sociable. I followed that pursuit in two ways, both of which led to eventual enforced resignations. One was the church choir and the other was the Boy Scouts.

The church was All Saints, in Old Swan. It was a nice little church with quite large gardens close to the primary school and I became after a period of service the Head Choirboy for which I was given a very small sum of money.

This was a pleasant choir, I would say, but of course involved rehearsals and frequent attendance at church. The reason for the dismissal or resignation arose because at that time the cinemas were closed on Sundays. There had been a campaign to open them which led to a decision to have a referendum so people could vote as to whether or not the cinemas were to open on a Sunday. For my part I was for the motion as it was a rare treat to go to the cinema in those days. Generally I could not go in the evenings as it was too late and of course I was at school most of the days. The choirboys all agreed to take the propaganda which had been put in all the pews and make aeroplanes out of it. The vicar wasn't at all pleased with this and decided not to pay us one month's choirboy fees. So the rebels then came to the surface and left under protest at not being paid.

Quite early on I was a Cub and later became a Scout and subsequently a patrol leader. This was during the time when Scout Masters had changed from being quite venerable gentlemen who hadn't been in the Services to those just leaving them. I'm not sure which of the two categories was most difficult to live with. One of the older ones simply had an over enthusiastic liking for the boys, who were all canny enough to stay as far away from him as possible, particularly during the camping weekends when he would invite one of us to join him in his relatively comfortable camp bed. He had very few takers, I assure you; we were a wily lot even at thirteen. My career in the Scouts came to a very early end. Scouts don't have Courts Martial, but if they did I would certainly have been a candidate.

My unfortunate premature departure from the Scouts arose from two incidents. The first was while camping with Patrol Leaders and senior Scouts at Burscough, some twelve miles outside Liverpool where we had our own tent which was left with the farmer. We would travel to Ormskirk, walk miles, erect the tent and enjoy ourselves throughout the weekend, returning on Sunday night. It was good fun. We were self-sufficient, taking our own food with us.

We arrived there one night to find that the tent was already erected, which we thought was rather fortunate because it was raining excessively. On arriving at it however we found it was occupied by Girl Guides and a very snooty Guide mistress. She adamantly refused to let us stay inside the tent in spite of the pouring rain on the grounds that Boy Scouts and Girl Guides should not sleep in a tent in the same field.

This was a regulation we had never heard of and anyway, at that age, we weren't interested in chasing girls or even, to be specific, wanting their company. We were told to go and sleep in the pig sty, which was empty of pigs but hardly the place to spend the night, particularly since there were holes in the roof. We put up with this for about an hour and then refused to accept it any longer; we barged into the tent and insisted on sleeping there. For this were were reported to the District Headquarters and reprimanded for un-Boy Scoutly behaviour.

The second and more serious incident occurred when we went with the younger boys to a summer camp called Loggerheads in North Wales. On that occasion a young Scout Master just out of the Services had just taken over and either he was trying to repeat his army experiences or he was a latent inherent bully. We put up with quite a bit of this until I and some of the senior Scouts took issue with him. His response was unpleasant. A short while afterwards we simply would not allow him to continue and took the younger Scouts home with us. That was the end of my Scouting career. A second reprimand led to dismissal and I went on to join the opposition – the Navy Cadets – which in the event was far more interesting to my personal inclination.

My demise with the Scouts was perhaps another example of the truculent obstinate side of my character, but also showed at quite a young age a serious social concern, one of equality and one of fairness. It was my misfortune to be reprimanded twice by the Scout headquarters for not behaving as they put it 'in the way of a patrol leader' which I was and should have done.

CHAPTER 2

The Early Years

THIS PERIOD BETWEEN fifteen and twenty-five was varied and interesting, perhaps even a kaleidoscope of experiences. Having completed the two year course at the Old Swan Technical Institute there was no formal way forward to University education save, as was the practice in those days, of paying for it or alternatively passing the Open University test.

Additionally there was little work in 1950 as the first effects of unemployment in the post war recession were beginning to appear; secondly, I was desperately short of personal finance; and thirdly, whilst the technical aspect of my education was quite satisfactory, the literary and other aspects were deficient.

This left me with the opportunity to pursue the only chance in front of me which was to enter into an electrical apprenticeship coupled with part-time studies at the Liverpool College of Technology. This was really six years of effective studies with practical education leaving me at worst a practising electrical technician or at best, which of course I aspired to, being a graduate electrical engineer.

The practical aspects of this work, inspection and design of medium to large electrical installations and assisting with the installation, were in themselves rewarding if not sometimes overwhelming. It gave me a very good understanding of the commercial/industrial activities in the Merseyside area.

For instance Merseyside was the second largest flour milling centre in the world with five or six major flour milling plants on the Wirral, all of which had been modernized, large-scale high-powered electrical motors driving the entire plants. All of these were re-designed and up-graded.

I was involved in inspecting public buildings such as the Law Courts and Philharmonic Hall, and, quite sadly, the mental institutions and old people's homes which were generally ex-workhouses, to ensure satisfactory standards were being maintained. Gasworks, commercial buildings, a whole variety of interesting projects were involved.

One in particular that gave cause for concern was the testing of Henderson's Department Store in Church Street. This was a six storey building owned by the House of Fraser. They had open staircases and a substantial number of major faults in electrical distribution and the wiring of the building. I recommended and assisted in the design which led to the complete re-wiring of the whole building.

This re-wiring subsequently took place under the direction of a different consultant and shortly after completion a fire broke out in Hendersons and a number of people, believed to be eleven, died as a consequence. An investigation was set up at St. George's Hall to decide the responsibility for this fire which, it was alleged, emanated from a large power cable entering the building not being properly installed. It seemed ironic that condemning the existing electrical installation in the building had led to a fairly new one which, it was suggested, was the original cause of the fire and subsequent loss of life.

My studies on the other hand were equally difficult, being part-time during the week and evening. The initial Ordinary National Certificate in Electrical Engineering followed four years of study. I succeeded in achieving a distinction in a subject which was possibly a complete waste of time, namely Direct Current Motors and Generators. I then took the Higher National Certificate which was fundamentally basic physics, electrical engineering, mathematics and associated subjects, which I think I just about passed by the time I had finished. But I still had to do two other subjects in order to graduate for the Institution of Electrical Engineers. One was English and the other one turned out to be Advanced Mathematics.

The English course consisted of studying the Civil Service Course in English and sitting the Civil Service examination. This is really something I should have done first, not last, as my long-founded fear of the use of English and my concern about my spelling difficulties arising from my speech impediment, were to some extent overcome by the intensive course for the Civil Service examination which I duly passed.

There was a delay in taking the final subject, Advanced Mathematics, as a consequence of a disruption to my career arising around the vagaries of the National Service Act which were at that stage going through a changing process.

In reality I worked as an electrical technician at AV Roe, having passed the Higher National Certificate, and did a short spell in the Merchant Navy before I finally studied and took the Advanced Mathematics Certificate at Manchester University to complete my Graduate examination.

It was all a time-consuming struggle against long hours of study, intensive work and the bureaucracy of the National Service that almost frustrated my ambition to qualify as an electrical engineer. No doubt it was character building, but at the time it was very hard work indeed.

During this period I had my first experience of the relationship between Government and industry. AV Roe was the aircraft manufacturer which subsequently became part of British Aerospace. This was in a new department headed by a chap named John Pilcher, which was involved in re-designing electrical systems on aircraft which were driven by alternating current, as opposed to the traditional direct current. I guess I was the second in John's small team of about six and he allowed me a fair degree of responsibility and involvement in this somewhat vital project.

AV Roe at the time was certainly one of Britain's, if not the world's, leading aircraft manufacturers. It had a long history to the AV Roe 504, which was one of the most successful early planes to fly in the First World War. Avro's great achievement was to design and build the Lancaster bomber, unaided by Government support and, some say, against opposition from the beginning of the war.

The in-house made, and privately built, Lancaster bomber was indeed an outstanding success, a major contributor to Britain's war against Germany. It succeeded the somewhat unsatisfactory 2-engined

Manchester bomber. I believe over ten thousand Lancasters were subsequently built, in the large AV Roe manufacturing organization. This bomber moved on to a derivative called the Shackleton which was in service until the 1980s or even possibly the 1990s but AV Roe's principal concern in my time was to design the Vulcan bomber.

The Ministry of Defence had commissioned three bombers, the Valiant, the Vulcan and the Victor. The Valiant was a Vickers bomber which was deemed to be an infill in the 1950s waiting the arrival of the Vulcan and subsequently, what it was believed to be the Ministry of Defence preferred choice the Valiant crescent wing shaped bomber.

The Vulcan itself was unique because it was the first full delta wing aircraft and clearly it was in competition with the Vickers Valiant, the main production order, to replenish the RAF's bomber fleet consisting mostly, as I have mentioned, of the Lancaster or its derivatives.

The Vulcan of course was also different. Apart from being the first V-shaped aircraft, it was also powered by jet engines. It was supposed to be capable of delivering hydrogen bombs at quite long ranges from the UK.

When I arrived they had built four mini-Vulcans which they called 707s, which were doing experimental aerodynamic trials on the performance of airflow over delta wing aircraft. They had built two prototype Vulcans, one the VX770 and the second the VX777. Both these aircraft had conventional direct current generating systems and all the problems associated with that kind of power supply.

One of the first six prototype production aircraft XA893 had been assigned for specific development of the alternating current system. We designed a test pack for the aircraft and the job our group was involved in was testing and developing. The real problem of developing alternating current systems on aircraft is that the alternators, or as they were then, generators, were powered by the engines, whose prime purpose of course was to fly the aircraft and therefore the relative speed of the engines was conditioned to the performance of the aircraft, not generating power.

This involved development of the variable gear device attached to the engine, which ensured that the speed of the output of the variable gear was the same from the four engines, and therefore it was possible to synchronize the four generators to produce the combined 240 KVA alternating current output. All the devices of course on the aircraft were also DC or associated with variable DC power supplies so it was necessary to have dummy loads on the aircraft to simulate the power requirements.

XA893 was therefore fitted out with jet engines which had both a generator and a variable speed gear device to drive an alternator. The bomb bay was full of test loads to create the load conditions that the aircraft would normally both on the ground and in flight have from its main electrical equipment.

We spent days and days and days on the ground setting up the aircraft which was a very interesting experience. When I get on an aircraft today I recall all the problems that one can encounter in the development phase and I listen to noises, in particular associated with electrical and mechanical devices, to see if I can assess that they are working.

Eventually we got the aircraft to a state of proper test flying and I had the exciting experience of being one of the five crew on the early test flights of XA893, which subsequently became the standard Vulcan in production. The Vulcan was in service possibly longer than most other bombers, although apart from the flights to the Falklands it never actually saw military action.

The ponderous bureaucratic process of the proceedings with regard to my deferment from National Service to allow my studies to continue, and the proper course of action to ensure that they could, arose one afternoon off the Pier Head in Liverpool when I called into Canadian Pacific to see whether there were any temporary offerings for electrical officers.

By good fortune the Chief Engineer whom I met had known my father who at one stage had been a Purser in the Canadian Pacific Line and was able to offer me an appointment subject to the usual credentials one needs from the Department of Transport to effect an appointment.

So very quickly I found myself moving from flying to sailing in ships. This was probably the part of my life when I began to realize there was more to life than long hard hours of study and endeavour. There was such a thing as fun and social interests. Being on those ships was like a holiday.

The duties of the electrical officer were to ensure any emergency could be handled with the staff at his disposal and to log any electrical or electronic defects to ensure that on arrival at port they could be rectified. This meant that most of the time there was nothing to do except stroll the decks, eat the rather wholesome and enjoyable food and meet the social company which was numerous, as the ship was principally involved in taking emigrants to Canada, people returning to Britain or members of the US personnel to North America and Rotterdam.

Canadian Pacific operated a number of cargo ships and liners from Europe to the east coast of America and Canada. The *Empress of France*, which I was particularly attached to, would do a series of runs to Boston, Halifax, Montreal or Quebec from Liverpool or Rotterdam depending on its destination. They were operating at a time when there were a great many American and Canadian troops in Europe and would carry large numbers of servicemen sailing to take up their duties in Europe or retuning at the end of their term.

One particular trip was quite interesting because there were about 700 passengers, somewhat short of the capacity of 800 the ship could carry, almost entirely women and children who were relatives of soldiers and officers serving in Europe. Why they should be chosen to sail all at the same time on the same ship I don't know, but nevertheless it was an unusual number of women and children to have on board, and it was a ten-day trip. It certainly increased the interest for the merchant sailors on board, and the social life was pretty good, I have to say without exaggerating. One particular difficulty arose, in that they had decided to put on board a large number of washing machines to augment the services that would normally be done by stewards and service people. About three days out from the coast it became apparent that the enormous volume of water we carried was being depleted very rapidly, at a much higher rate than usual. Water on a ship acts as ballast to a certain extent and quite a large proportion is not drinking water but is kept permanently in tanks. It is seldom replaced, so cannot be used for drinking water and in this case there was a small drought on board. So for ten hours a day it was not permitted for water to be consumed for anything other than drinking and necessary health purposes. Drinking water wasn't in fact available in the cabins, so it was quite an interesting restriction placed on passengers and crew. I'm not quite sure who handled the ladies who didn't care for this restriction very much, but certainly there was some interesting dialogue between the pursers, front officers and staff and the ladies who wished to have more baths than the ship's crew, or the Captain at any rate, thought he could accommodate.

It was a good life. I met many people and enjoyed it enormously. It left me with a sense of freedom in a number of ways. One was enjoyment of social company. Another of course was the discovery of foreign lands: Canada, USA and continental Europe.

This wasn't to last too long as I was required to return to complete my studies at Manchester University, having now been given the exemption requested of the Department of National Service.

Canadian Pacific was a fine company with a fine tradition. They were keen to have me stay with them and offered to pay me during my studies and treat me in effect as an officer ashore on study. Unfortunately as the particular syllabus and course did not fit into anything that the Ministry of Transport deemed appropriate for the Merchant Navy, the Department of National Service threatened me that unless I formally left Canadian Pacific and the Navy then my exemption would automatically be withdrawn if I was ashore for more than four weeks or so.

Hence I was unemployed but nonetheless able to pursue my studies which I successfully completed within a year and got my graduation, by which time the armed forces did not wish to avail themselves of my services and I was in the position of wondering what would be the next step.

This led to my first term of employment with Plessey which lasted about three years, although at that time the company wasn't called Plessey. It was the Automatic Electric Telephone Company and I took up a design engineering position with the so-called Supervisory and Remote Control Division, a division that concerned itself with the centralised control of large networks, in particular power and rail networks. I assisted in the design of controls and remote instrumentation for the national grid network and was subsequently assigned as the project engineer for the electrification programme for British Railways, which was trialled between Manchester and Crewe, and subsequently expanded to include Glasgow, Liverpool and Euston.

This involved a number of control centres, the first one being a trial of electric traction between Manchester and Crewe. It was interesting work. Instead of being on planes and boats, I now found myself on trains. There was an affinity of interest in travel and the workings of the railways, steam of course still being predominant although diesel was also a major source of traction which I found very much to my liking.

The system had a major control room at Crewe which switched all the heavy 25,000 volt power network between Liverpool and Manchester and Stafford to ensure continuity of power or removal of power for maintenance or emergency services. It also controlled the flow of power between the various power lines to ensure the network was properly balanced for the purpose of electrical locomotives proceeding smoothly on their journey.

There was one particular innovation in this, which was quite a responsible and important decision British Railways made at what I believe was Board level. With a 25,000 volt overhead power, supply unknown in Britain hitherto but widely used in France, the dangers of vandals throwing wires from bridges and short circuiting it could be quite serious. More particularly, loss of power through temporary interruption could not be left until inspection, otherwise there would be frequent disruption to the trains.

So the decision was made that any interruption to power would automatically, through the supervisory and control system, put 25,000 volts back on the line. This was to be repeated three times until the power had tripped out three times and then manual inspection had to be made of the line where the fault had appeared. Not to do this would have meant possible frequent interruptions to the train services by vandals. However, automatically to restore power could result in a potential threat to life following a crash or derailment of a train which brought the power lines down with it and exposed the people to electrocution from this very high voltage.

It was a difficult decision and we took a small supervisory control diagram of control equipment to British Railways headquarters to demonstrate this working and the arguments to the Board. The decision of course was a British Railways decision. They, in the event, decided to have automatic reconnection three times of the 25,000 volts overhead supply to provide as far as practical a non interrupted service. I feel over the period of time that this was a brave but correct decision in terms of continuity of rail service. In today's climate would they make the same decision? I doubt it.

We had installed the Manchester/Crewe system and commissioned it and the rest was only reproducing the proven system. At this stage I decided that I wanted broader horizons. I think I was becoming disenchanted with career prospects at the Automatic Telephone Electric Company and made a move for a position in London which really led directly into my computer period.

Incidentally the Automatic Telephone Electric Company, being Britain's largest telecommunications manufacturer, was taken over at the same time as Ericsons of Nottingham, another major manufacturer, by the then much smaller Plessey Group. I am not sure that this in the end was a helpful takeover and when I returned to Plessey, of which the Automatic Electric Telephone company was now a major part, some many years later there had been very few signs of any constructive change to the Company itself.

CHAPTER 3

Computers

WITHOUT QUESTION my most formative years were when I was working in the new and fast-growing computer industry. I shall cover this section in two parts, the first concerned with the time up to about 1970 and then a section called 'the ICL experience', dealing with the attempted restructuring of the computer industry.

Sperry Univac

In the latter part of 1959 I had taken a written examination followed by an interview given by the Sperry Rand Corporation to select two candidates to study computers in Switzerland.

I had reached the position working in Liverpool, perhaps influenced by my spell in the Merchant Navy, when I knew that there had to be bigger horizons and more interesting activities away from Merseyside, and I had been pursuing work particularly in London for some time.

I was appointed on 1 January 1960 as Design Engineer for John Brown Construction, then based in Paddington, London, who had obtained contracts to build at least one power station in Russia.

When I arrived at John Brown I met no one whom I had met at the interview, and I was advised that they required me to be a draughtsman, as they put it 'to establish my capabilities'. I was expecting to take up a position as a design engineer and was distinctly unhappy at this surprising turn of events. I spent the morning contemplating the prospect of leaving and finding myself unemployed in what to me at that time was quite a strange city, London.

I had nearly reached this decision when I decided to call my mother to tell her what I was doing, from a phone box outside work. When I rang she told me that there was a letter waiting for me which had been there for a few days and I asked her to open and read it. Inside was the offer from Sperry Rand to study computers in Switzerland, but I had to reply that day and travel to Switzerland almost immediately. This extraordinary coincidence could not have come at a better time. I immediately rang Sperry Rand and told them I wanted to take up the position and was available that week and would they send me instructions as to where I had to report in Switzerland. I went out and had a pint of bitter by myself to celebrate my good fortune.

I was not at that stage even concerned about the financial aspects, although it turned out that the generosity of Sperry Rand was such that the package was worth more than I was going to be paid by John Brown. So after two hours to build up my courage I went back to John Brown and insisted on meeting, immediately, the Chief Engineer and Head of Personnel who had actually interviewed me. It clearly was unusual at the time for a new recruit to insist on such a course of action.

I told them that I really did not want to work there. I wanted, in view of the fact that they had misled me about the job I thought I was taking, that we should call it a day and I should simply just not start. The Chief Engineer and the Head of Personnel were clearly embarrassed by this whole episode and the fourth member of the meeting, who was my new boss, was clearly their source of embarrassment. The three tried to ward off my leaving but within an hour I was out and free and looking forward to my exciting move to Switzerland.

A few words about Sperry Rand could be of interest. In the 1950s the Sperry Rand Corporation had been created by the merger of the Sperry Corporation and Remington Rand. On the face of it there was a great deal of logic in this merger. Remington was the largest office equipment manufacturer in the world and had a division known as the Univac Computing Division, which at that stage was the largest computer manufacturer but which had failed to exploit this technical advantage commercially. They needed support to market the product but the worlds of typewriters and computers were too far apart.

Sperry on the other hand was the major US defence contractor and possibly the world's largest company in the field of navigation, having developed the Sperry gyroscope way back in the twenties and probably every aircraft flying in the western world had one on board. They were of course in the field of guided missiles and other defence activities, the vanguard of technological development.

So this merger on paper seemed ideal, a company with a worldwide marketing organization in office equipment backed with competence in large computers which even IBM did not hold at that stage, and massive defence contracts at the very boundaries of expansion of computerized development. But like all arranged marriages the psychology of the senior management was the exact opposite. Old man Rand had not exactly been clear as to what was useful and what was obsolete in the inventory and Sperry had clearly not been prepared for the mysteries of mass marketing on an international scale.

In addition the Sperry Rand Corporation owned a company called Vickers, which was an hydraulic company and came with a very large market share in hydraulic mechanisms which did not fit in with the rest, and Remington Shavers, which had no relationship whatsoever with the main activities of the Sperry Rand organization. There was a further division called New Holland, a major world player in non-tractor farm implements, harvesters for example. The situation got quite desperate in terms of the liquidity of Sperry Rand. Harry Vickers, from Vickers, emerged as a new rather placid but determined Chairman endeavouring to do his very best to consolidate these disparate enterprises.

My studies in Switzerland were concerned with the workings of the then latest, but now very obsolete, computer, the so-called Univac Solid State 80, which was a direct derivative of the first computer, the Eniac, developed by Massachusetts Institute of Technology. The proof of success was at the end of the studies, for Sperry offered me proper employment and career prospects.

The other students were interesting. There were two from each European country although the other person from Britain happened to be an Indian. They were a very fine fraternity, particularly the Dutch, German, Austrian and Italian delegates. I enjoyed it all immensely: the fascination of the studies of computers in their infancy and the chance to meet Europeans who fortunately nearly all spoke English, although the dominant second language tended to be German as we were in Zurich. I spoke no French and struggled somewhat to learn some basic German.

During this period I spent time in Austria and Germany. Both countries, particularly Germany, were already considerably ahead of the UK in the application of computers. Then in mid-1961 I returned to the UK to endeavour to install the first Sperry Rand Univac computer in the UK. This turned out to be an interesting but exhausting experience.

The reliability of these devices in those days was far from satisfactory. Indeed the night before I married my first wife, I worked until 4 a.m. to try and get the first computer working, which was incidentally based at Remington Rand headquarters in Holborn, London.

I married Pat on 24 August 1961 in Runcorn in Cheshire. In some ways it typified my way of life at the time. The church was on the top of a hill overlooking the ICI Runcorn works; to its left could be seen the Shell Oil refinery and fronting both plants was the wide expanse of the River Mersey. The reception was held at the local hostelry, almost mandatory for people getting married in Runcorn.

Partly through my fault we did not have sufficient cars to take the guests from the church to the reception so twenty-eight guests were left there, eventually travelling on a double decker bus. My parents were part of the stranded group and my father was very proud of the twenty-eight 3d. tickets he had paid for. A wedding is generally considered to be the bride's day but to me too it was a significant milestone. It was the last occasion I spent any time with the friends I had been with so much during my teens and early twenties.

My separation from my married existence was for a large part to continue for the next thirty years. People who wish to pursue careers in industry and commerce pay a high personal price. They very seldom have sufficient time left to spend with their families. On reflection a selfish attitude, but nevertheless, in spite of the fact that sacrifice is not recognized by the public, if people weren't prepared to do it there would be little economic or, consequentially, social development.

These early computer installations were based on a solid state device called germanium, which unlike silicon was very highly temperature sensitive and relied on a tightly controlled air conditioning to ensure no variation in temperature, otherwise the devices would suffer from a defect called thermal shock. Thermal shock would damage the devices and consequently the computer would fail.

Silicon was then on the horizon and indeed silicon overcame the problems with germanium, but the learning process was invaluable both in the design of the chips themselves and more particularly in the importance of the development of the driving engine in any computer, namely the software.

The most interesting installation about that time was at Coutts Bank. Coutts was, and is, a wholly owned subsidiary of National Westminster Bank, of which I was, on two occasions, a director. The Coutts clientele had high incomes or historic wealth, and were small in number but very demanding in terms of service. It used to call itself the Queen's Bank. I have no idea whether the Queen has her account there or not, but that was the claim that used to be associated with it, particularly bearing in mind that it was also claimed to be the oldest existing bank in England.

The point about Coutts is they weren't prepared even in early 1960 to give their customers computer print-outs that simply had numbers on. They wanted, and insisted, that all the computer print-outs on the customers' accounts were, as they put it, fully descriptive, listing all the cheque transactions. That was a level of service that even today very few banks achieve. They still do not provide fully descriptive statements, principally because of cost rather than technology. The second condition, however, that they laid down was that owing to the confidentiality of the bank they would not allow an outside company to write or test the program, or handle the data. This of course was impracticable. We were not completely excluded but nevertheless they insisted that very largely the people involved in the project were their own banking staff, trained to program and operate the computer.

The project was a great success. Many of the contemporary failures in computing were really arising because customers simply said, 'I want a computer to do this,' and left the supplier to cobble up whatever sort of program he thought appropriate. Almost invariably this was not satisfactory, hence the computer system failed. But the staff at Coutts appeared to grasp the art of designing computer programs, and built into them all the special techniques and know-how that they themselves had.

In designing the programs the system was replicated by the computer when it was processing the information that they, and members of their staff, had been processing. It worked very well. Indeed I could understand, on observing some of the print-outs, why they wanted the matter to be of the utmost discretion. If only, and I have said this many times, other companies would have adopted the same policy there would have been far fewer failures in the early computer days and the industry would have advanced at an even faster rate than it did.

As we moved to the mid-60s it became apparent that the merger between Sperry and Univac in particular was going to pay real dividends. The communications knowledge of Sperry and the computing developments of Univac were unquestionably complementary. Univac began to develop what was known as the 1100 series, which to this day is one of the most powerful large scale commercial computers available.

The 1100 series in this first version had a so-called thin film memory which is a very fast memory technique, subsequently dropped because of cost but nevertheless totally reliable and effective in its time. It also had on-line communication ability and even better multi-processor developments. Input/Output Units were coupled together and handled data in a way previously never considered possible.

The first customer in Britain to take an interest in this was the Royal Air Force, not for military reasons but for administrative purposes, in their Pay and Records Department. After a great deal of investigation – at this stage I was spending a lot of time in the United States – the RAF convinced the Central Branch of the Government, the Civil Service Agency, that the 1107 was the only computer that would meet their needs.

This was embarrassing as at the time great emphasis was being put on placing computer orders from the many British companies then in computer manufacture. That the RAF should for commercial, performance and operational reasons, decide that the 1107 was substantially better was not taken easily by the then Labour Government who did not want to be seen to be supporting American products, regardless of how advanced they were.

This was a difficult and demanding project, not least because the facilities built by the Ministry of Works and Public Buildings did not perform to the specification required for the environment of the computer. After a great deal of effort the system was finally commissioned almost on the same day that my twin daughters were born in the middle of 1965.

There was no turning back for Univac in the United Kingdom after that breakthrough. The next major contract was the National Engineering Laboratory, which again was a Government Agency, who again insisted on in this case the Univac 1106. This was a cheaper version but the only computer in the world that had the capacity and ability to communicate major displays and interact with engineers so that more rapid design could be achieved in the various engineering projects the NEL was working on.

This was even less acceptable to the Government who at this stage, following Wilson's famous statement about 'the searing white heat of technology', had appointed Frank Cousins to be the first Secretary of State for Technology. Frank's very first announcement was that NEL would acquire this Univac equipment. It was not known whether he knew it at the time but as he was promoting British technology he was announcing a major step forward with totally American technology.

Other important contracts followed. Shell, which had been almost exclusively IBM, decided to trial the large scale Univac 1108. This was done in a garage because no other space was available at the time and they had some tremendous problems with the software, but finally it worked and Shell moved substantially to the 1108. And so indeed did BP (British Petroleum) as did their sister company, then Shellmex and BP Distributor Company. It was a rapidly growing population of large scale computers in Britain, and we had become a serious threat to all the other computer manufacturers and suppliers, including IBM who at that stage had grabbed a large section of the information technology market through its punch card and small computer applications.

Towards the end of the 60s, when I had held the position of Director of Engineering and then Director of Systems, American firms kept on appointing American Managing Directors. This I disliked. I therefore decided in fact to join a large group of other Univac people who had gone to a company called Mohawk Data Sciences. Mohawk, or MDS as it was called, was in fact a separate company but acted almost as a subsidiary to Univac. MDS specialised in data capture and printer output. It was another fast growth company, in Europe as well as in the United States. They made me the Managing Director in the United Kingdom, a position which I enjoyed for two years, and which gave me the first insight into the minds of senior political figures. This insight came, in particular, by meeting John Stonehouse who at the time was the Minister for the Post Office. I was to meet John later, but after this short experience with MDS, Univac wanted me to come back to run the British company as the Managing Director. This became a most exciting period.

Sperry Univac large scale computers were working well, whilst IBM decided to relaunch a whole new product line. IBM's plans were over ambitious and they were having desperate problems with the medium and large scale computers. Additionally, the now rationalized British computer industry's product was obsolete.

It gave me a wonderful opportunity. We were taking orders from large scale computer systems, at least once a month. They would come in from sectors of British Industry that previously we would never have been able to penetrate. The building societies for instance with Abbey National and Nationwide; the County Councils with Surrey and Westminster; the hospitals with London and Birmingham; and further penetration into the heart of Government activity was in the form of a major system being ordered by the Treasury.

It was an exhilarating period of business success and technological development. It led to a number of things, in particular to being noticed by the competitors having a desire to talk to us, and the Government, particularly Kenneth Baker and Nick Ridley. I had my early meetings with them while they were in opposition although Kenneth Baker, when the Conservatives came back to run the Government, was to hold a critical position in the development of computers. Nick Ridley subsequently played a major political role in the country.

About this time I was also seconded to three other international activities. One was the world wide installation at US Air Force bases of a common computer system, of which a number came to Britain.

The second was the NASA programme which extended beyond the States, in fact covering the whole world in terms of communications and computers, and I had the opportunity to be involved in that very exciting project. It was a tremendous insight into the abilities of the Americans when they really set their mind to organizing things and getting them done quickly.

I think there can be no finer example of effective management than 25,000 people being recruited over a short period of time by NASA, in effect to put one man on the moon. There were 25,000 disparate individuals from different backgrounds with different cultures and from different disciplines, all working together for the one common cause: to bring together the resources and put one man on the moon at a point in time.

The story I am told, which I am sure is a fable, is that President

Kennedy, when he was in power in the early sixties, sent for the head of NASA which was then quite a small department considering and studying the implications of aviation and science in space. The dialogue then went the following way:

The executive responsible for NASA of course was quite astonished by being called to see the President and the President said to him, 'Can you put a man on the moon within the next four years?' The NASA chief said, 'Well, I suppose with the right resources we can do it, Mr President,' and returned to see his staff. He told them the question he had been asked and said that he had to respond to it formally. His staff by and large agreed that it was possible and one chap said, 'Of course, I hope the President doesn't expect us to bring him back as well.' Nonetheless, joking aside, Kennedy's dream was realized, regrettably after his death.

The last international programme was SITA. SITA stands for Sociétié Internationale Télégraphe Aeronautique which is a world-wide body run from Paris, responsible for all inter airline and inter country communications, over and above the sovereign states of the individual countries in terms of control over their telegraphy. SITA switched millions of messages per day through the world and wanted to computerize the whole programme. We were successful and organized from London a fair number of difficult meetings, trying to enjoin American culture and British interests and French suspicions to acquire what was then probably the world's largest commercial computer order ever placed, all of which turned out quite satisfactorily.

Then we turned our attention to other technology companies. I joined in discussions with other computer companies and senior members of the Government. Two of these were successful. The first was the acquisition of SAAB computing from the SAAB parent company in Scandinavia. SAAB had been having some difficulties funding the research and development on computers and on advanced military aircraft, and decided on some sort of collaborative activity. After a fair number of meetings in the UK, Sweden and USA and with the bankers Wallenbergs who had great influence over the control of

SAAB, it was finally agreed that they would exchange their interests for a consideration to be under the control of Univac. That arrangement blossomed with the new Univac product and a very well established Scandinavian market, and the business grew from strength to strength.

Likewise in Brazil, Siemens had some doubts about their computer activities in the country. From a contact in Germany I had discussions in the USA and Univac again took over Siemens in Brazil. During this period I got to know some very interesting people. Just to mention a few: firstly Eddie Nixon who at that stage was the Chairman/Chief Executive of IBM UK. Whilst there were no prospects of any business relationship between us other than the competitive relationship that existed, he kept in touch from time to time and I have known him and seen him frequently ever since. Eddie was an example of a real hard worker who would return on an overnight flight from the States and continue working in his office on an almost routine basis.

Sir Jack Cohen, founder of Tesco, was intrigued with what Carrefour, the French supermarket, was doing and visualised, with his outstanding foresight, the supermarket developments in the UK. At that stage the supermarket programme had not started. Jack's main concern was the logistics of handling the large volumes of stock rapidly. He would from time to time invite me to join him at his Regent's Park home for coffee in his office or in a club in London to sound out his thinking. He understood that supermarkets could only function if the technology base could be built to create the foundations. He was a man of outstanding ability. It is easy to understand why he was able to create the foundation to make Tesco the company that it is today.

There were two ladies at the time who impressed me enormously, both American. Ann Whiting was our communications PR lady. I do not know the details but she had had a very sad personal experience. She was the first public relations individual I had met and a real character; for instance when talking of advertising she would say, 'No naked ladies, let's get to the message.' I have to this day copies of advertisements that we did at the time creating purposes and uses of computers which were way ahead of their time in terms of placing the message to the potential interested party. Ann died while we were still colleagues, quite young. I felt her a very sad loss indeed.

The other was Commander Grace Hopper, also an extraordinary person. Grace was a senior officer in the US Navy by virtue of her computer competence. She was, I am told, the designer of COBAL, the first computer compiling language that eliminated the need to understand numbers to program the computer. You programmed it in English. She was always at the forefront of technology and was to be of great assistance to the US Navy and indeed played a part in the development of the micro-chip. She had a wonderful way of explaining herself to the public and I met her frequently on her trips to England and occasionally in America. Grace died about seven or eight years ago.

Eniac, as I mentioned earlier, was claimed to be the first pro-grammed electronic computer and subsequently led to the develop-ment of Univac. The designers were Echert and Maucly. I met both from time to time. It was interesting to know that in a sense each of them fulfilled some purpose in this vast industry, that they had laid the very foundations of developments in computing, and left others to carry it forward.

In attempting to understand the mentality of Government in relation to the understanding of technology I had a very valuable meeting with Airey Neave. I have mentioned earlier my luncheon with John Stonehouse. During the early 70s I saw Stonehouse on a number of occasions. He was interested, I think, in becoming a consultant for Univac, particularly internationally. Although a Member of Parliament, he was no longer a member of the Cabinet. As he put it, he was more effective outside the Cabinet and was involved in very complicated international trading activities.

During late 1974 and early 1975 I had the honour to be the Faraday Lecturer. The Faraday Lecture commemorates the great inventor Michael Faraday to whom is attributed the discovery of how to generate electricity and a variety of other important scientific discoveries in the early nineteenth century. It is organized by the Institution of Electrical Engineers and has been taking place over many

Prior to the 1st Faraday Lecture, REME Barracks, Hampshire, August 1974.

years. The lecture tours the country and is given in 16 locations: for instance, Newcastle, Leicester, Sheffield, Liverpool, Manchester, London, Belfast, Birmingham, Bristol, Southampton, and of course a number in London.

The lecture is repeated at least once in those locations, sometimes as many as three times, the repeats principally for the benefit of school-children. My deputy lecturer and assistant was Dr Malachy McIntyre. We together wrote the lecture and devised the supporting films, slides and demonstrations, and we split the lecturing between us, myself tending to do the evening lecture and Dr McIntyre carrying out the afternoon lectures to the schoolchildren.

Faraday was a remarkable man and to understand and get the feel for the lecture it is almost mandatory that you study the nature of the person himself. He had no education and made all his discoveries by the process of experimentation although he had been a pupil under some earlier nineteenth century research workers. Much of his work took place at the Royal Institution and indeed there is still today a replica of the laboratory where he made his profound and important discoveries. He believed that an inventor did not understand what he was doing or the results of his work unless he could explain them to children. There is much truth in this assertion. However complex the task, unless you explain it to children you don't understand the fundamental concept of the subject.

He initiated the Children's Lectures which take place at the Royal Institution every Christmas, given by an eminent scientist of the day who explains what he is doing to an audience of children. This programme is televised. The Faraday Lectures themselves, as I have explained, tour the country and the lecturer and his assistant probably lecture to about 100,000 people in the process of that lecture tour.

My subject was the use of computers. It was the second Faraday Lecture covering computers, but the first one had dealt with the way computers worked. Mine dealt with their use, in particular how computers were programmed to make them operate in the solution of problems. The second section showed a variety of applications in various industries and the third section was looking into the future and home shopping, remote banking, air traffic control and the proposition of Internet type activities, all of which of course have been put into practice within the last ten years or so.

It was an interesting experience because whilst the lecture was always the same, the audience reaction in the various halls was very different. For instance the lecture in Stoke fell on stone cold silence. You tend to react to the audience in terms of how good or bad you are on the night. The lecture in Southampton got into catastrophic problems when the equipment broke down which led to a half hour break in the middle of it. The lectures in Bristol, and in particular Liverpool and Birmingham, were extremely well received, with a strong enthusiastic audience response.

It is particularly poignant that the lecture in Birmingham was the first major public event which had taken place since the Birmingham bomb. There was a high degree of apprehension in the City Hall before the lecture, which somehow or other was dispelled as it proceeded. In the end there was almost a feeling of relief that there had been an important public meeting following a major atrocity. The Lord Mayor at the lecture demonstrably appreciated and enjoyed the whole proceedings.

The ICL Saga

This case study is an example of the difficulties of two companies attempting to join together to capitalize on each other's technology and rationalize their marketing against a near monopoly supplier.

The political desire to maintain control over a struggling company and the influence of Brussels even in the 70s torpedoed any prospect of a realistic merger.

In the early 70s the Univac Division of Sperry Rand had been so successful it probably accounted for half the total company's revenue. It had been particularly successful in the UK, taking a major section of the large machine computer base. Some diehards stood out with IBM but many moved across to Univac equipment. It was only a question of time before the twenty or so computer manufacturers would be rationalized to a much smaller number.

Univac's fortunes were indeed going well. It had made a strategic computer acquisition – RCA computers which many had believed would be too difficult for Univac to handle, as the architecture of RCA computers was different from the Univac 1100 series. But handle it they did and well. They integrated the RCA customer base very quickly into the Univac customer base with a very high degree of customer satisfaction. Indeed RCA would have been unlikely to have survived had this transaction not taken place.

So there we were, the Number 2 computer company in the world making a rapid market growth in Europe, America and Japan. The successful acquisition of RCA Computers, consolidated in 1972 and 1973, led to a study into the merging of Univac with ICL, which was Britain's only remaining computer manufacturer and substantially bigger than its European counterparts. The first idea was to merge ICL and Univac UK. Subsequently the discussions developed into a proposed merger across Europe.

Let me touch upon some of the key personalities in all these discussions.

In Univac the key man was its President, Jerry Prost, a conservative Mormon with a highly technical background and not enthusiastic about corporate change. His Executive Vice President Harry Steinberg was an individual with immense vision and strong commercial drive but no technical knowledge, a man of dedication. Indeed the kind of leader you naturally wished to admire and support.

This made for a good combination – the conservatism of the President Prost and the drive and ambition of the Executive Vice-President Steinberg. At ICL there was Tom Hudson the Chairman, who had for many years been the chairman of IBM UK and had been elected into the ICL position as a consequence of being a Board member representing the Plessey Company, who were a major shareholder.

Tom's No. 2 was Arthur Humphreys, a large and lively character and enormous fun to be with socially, liked if not loved by the members of ICL with whom he had worked for or with over many years.

The Chief Executive of ICL at the time was Jeff Cross, who had recently left Univac and to avoid any complications was never involved in the discussions.

The two major shareholders at the time were GEC and Plessey, GEC because it had merged part of its English Electric activities into ICL and a balancing shareholding which Plessey had acquired after discussions with the Government, both of which were about 17.5 per cent of the company.

The dominant force in GEC was Sir Arnold Weinstock, later Lord Weinstock. He called himself the Managing Director but he was the Chief Executive. In Plessey it was Sir John Clark who was their chairman.

In the Government we had the principal minister the Rt. Hon.

Chris Chataway, who was a Minister for Industry, assisted by a number of very senior Civil Servants among whom were Ivor Manley and Larrie Tindale.

S.G. Warburg, the merchant bankers, played a key role largely because of the influence and contacts of Mr Henry Grundfelt, a memorable and distinguished member of that company.

On the European side Mr Ronnie Grierson, later Sir Ronald, was the Director General of the Commission for Industry. Later he became a Board member of the GEC Company.

The beginnings of this dialogue were two meetings in January 1972 with me and Arthur Humphries (ICL). First there was a discussion on the rationalization of the industry and the recognition that everybody was now talking to almost everybody else.

A more tangible statement came at the second meeting when Arthur said it was his firm belief that the strength of IBM and its dominant market position could only be challenged by a second force. That second force should include as far as possible all the other computer companies and he even had a name for it. It was the International Computer Company. There were a number of meetings in June that year beginning with me meeting Jerry Prost in Philadelphia and discussing the concept of a multi-national high technology company starting with Univac and ICL forming two new companies, one for marketing the computer products worldwide and the other for manufacturing and development.

Owing to the fact that the ICL situation was heavily underwritten by Government money and indeed that shareholders were pushing for more Government support, it was decided that the best course of action was for me to meet with members of the Government.

I met with Ivor Manley and his boss Richard Bullock in the same month and placed before them a number of important considerations: the need for effective competition against IBM, the value of Univac's acquisition of the RCA customer base and what we had done with it; the significance of Univac's No. 2 world position in computing; our idea of ICL's problems as they were seen particularly by their competitors; a proposal for a future association between Univac and ICL, two companies – one manufacturing and research and the second marketing. We drew out further detail such as that ICL would manufacture products for Univac in Europe and both companies would agree which was the stronger in individual countries with regard to the marketing company.

Immediately afterwards the Central Computer Agency, which is part of the Civil Service Department, asked to meet with me as all Government Departments like to be equally briefed, even though of course they brief each other.

I reported back to Gerry Prost and Harry Steinberg in early July and it was agreed, following what appeared to be encouraging Government reaction, we should orchestrate meetings with ICL.

In early July with Tom Hudson I set up the meeting which took place on 11 July at the Savoy Hotel between Gerry Prost (Univac), Tom Hudson (ICL) and Arthur Humphries (ICL). It was a good amiable sort of meeting and achieved what best it could. ICL were concerned about control not leaving the UK. Univac said that the best way to handle a problem was to break it down into sectors such as marketing, R & D and manufacturing and study them separately.

This was becoming a hot issue inside Government. Kenneth Baker, now Lord Baker, the then Minister for the Civil Service Department, together with his Civil Servants Mr Bullock and Mr Manley, met with me to be brought up to date and a meeting followed almost immediately with Chris Chataway and Jack Rampton (Department of Trade and Industry), the Permanent Under Secretary, at which we reviewed the Univac approach in Japan, which was a joint company as opposed to a subsidiary and was operating in fact in a very competitive way in Japan.

We discussed how this could be applied to discussions taking place with ICL and Univac. Meetings then took place with Tom Hudson and Arthur Humphries, who clearly resented the direct approach we made to the British Government. In a new situation, it doesn't matter where you start, you will always put somebody's nose out of joint, and clearly the approach to the Government had stimulated Tom and Arthur to prompt further debate. They made their position quite clear to me and it was very helpful. They were keen on a series of cross licences for Univac's technology. The only problem was that Univac's small systems, at that stage, were selling much better and subsequently ICL took on Univac's small systems and sold them under their own badge.

We discussed the R & D development continuing in the UK; the position of Government security because ICL was a prime supplier, or the preferred supplier, of British Government being a British company; how joint marketing might work; what cash could be required; ownership issues; and who would the management be.

I took this back and Univac then developed what it described as a series of indispensables, in other words deal busters – things that had to be met. This is really when the main policy of Sperry Rand Corporation and Univac emerged. It accepted from the outset that the majority ownership should reside in the United Kingdom. This was quite a significant concession and was based on the Japanese experience of having minority ownership in the country, and the business doing so well.

Univac was concerned about two things. One was that after the RCA experience there had to be strong product management. The company's products were to be merged quickly and effectively for the efficiencies and technical benefits that would bring.

Secondly they had a very poor opinion of the financial competence of ICL management and therefore they believed they should control the financial management. In other words they wanted management control, but were prepared to accept foreign ownership which could intercede with the management if it believed it was not acting purely in British interests.

It wanted Univac to merge into ICL's name; it wanted agreement in principle on product lines to avoid conflict; it was happy to accept a 40 per cent interest in the ownership and was quite unconcerned about the Board structure.

It wanted an initial order from ICL equal to half the volume that

Univac in the UK could sell at that point in time; such a discussion would almost certainly damage Univac's prospects to achieve sales when it came into the public arena.

Meanwhile word was passed to us that there wasn't really a lot of value in talking to Tom Hudson because, I do not know under what circumstances, the proposal was that Lord Kearton would assume the chair of ICL. Kearton at the time made his name by his stalwart defence of the ICI bid for Courtaulds.

It was suggested that we should spend more time with the principal shareholders, to convince them. None of this we particularly liked. There were too many people involved in discussions which almost certainly means you will never get a decision and furthermore there were strong shades of discord amongst shareholders and directors.

Nevertheless we did, and one principal shareholder we spoke to was GEC which had 17.5 per cent of ICL. In early September I met the then Sir Arnold, now Lord Weinstock, for whom I have the greatest of respect although that was not necessarily formed at the first meeting. Arnold's general thrust was that he didn't particularly like the Americans; ICL needed new management, a change of chairman, change of executive management. He made an astonishing statement to me that market share was not important to profit. It went against all my experience and education. Maybe we were talking about different things at the time.

He clearly did not have an understanding of the nature of the computer product and was talking very generally in this area. He certainly sowed the seeds of doubt about Tom Hudson's security and hinted that of course everything can be sold at its price. He suggested we didn't waste time talking about technical matters but should see what we had in mind by way of buying out his investment in ICL. In other words his main thrust was one of corporate commercial interest, not industrial strategy.

He said he had had discussions with Clancy Spangle who was then head of Honeywell, another possible suitor for ICL, and left me with the distinct impression that he was overreacting or alternatively could be a very difficult man to form any sort of relationship with, whether as an employee, partner or anything else.

The Government subsequently confirmed a few days later that Honeywell were indeed interested and had made some sort of approach. At the same meeting there was a fair amount of to-ing and fro-ing of who was being helpful and who was trying to hinder the approach. In other words our suspicions regarding the complexities of discussions creating difficulties were bearing fruit.

Gerry Prost and Harry Steinbeck came over and took considerable advice in terms of the legal and technical aspects of such a merger and largely they were no worse than what they would be in the States but were less well defined.

This cleared the way for the realization of a prospective merger.

Gerry Prost then met Sir Arnold Weinstock and formed the same impression as myself, and then we went on to have another key meeting with ICL in London in the early part of September. Present at this meeting were the two representatives of the DTI. Univac stressed from the outset that it didn't particularly like all these complex ownership issues and Government involvement and much preferred a mutually desirable and agreeable relationship and hoped that was what ICL and Univac would work towards.

The questions of management were really of concern about positions in all this – who would be Chairman, Chief Executive, and other appointments. These matters often defeat sensible mergers and are best dealt with at the beginning. If you can get out of the way who is going to be boss of what, then it often makes a smoother way for discussion on important corporate issues.

Discussion took place on marketing: in what country and how much money would be required, who would put in the money. Indeed it was a long useful meeting, Tom Hudson expressing his concerns. He was worried about the control of the research and development and did not want it exported from Britain. This would be a Government point of view. He was relaxed about the management and the ownership. He wished to know if Siemens or C2I, the French company, could be brought in. Univac agreed they could. Indeed it looked altogether a very positive meeting which would be followed by ICL putting down its indispensables or deal breakers. The two Boards would attempt within six months to reach a substantial agreement and study groups would be set up on a marketing, engineering, software development, finance and marketing support service.

Separate meetings took place with Sir John Clark, the chairman of Plessey, who hinted at the security of tenure of Tom Hudson and very much wanted the scene arranged so Plessey Telecommunications Technology and manufacturing ability could be brought into the equation.

This in a sense was all very helpful stuff and was quite different from the nature of the discussions taking place with the ICL principals. However a long meeting took place with Tom Hudson and Arthur Humphries, the DTI representatives, in the middle of September 1972. It was clear at this meeting that Tom Hudson's card had been marked by the Government and that the indispensables were really that UK must retain the ability to design substantial systems. Furthermore they must retain a major manufacturing presence in Europe. ICL believed that they should market all of Europe plus the Commonwealth with exclusive rights. An underwritten condition was that Univac's interests would never exceed 50 per cent of the ownership. The research by the combined company never would fall below the 6 per cent of revenue point. There clearly was a Government idea for an executive committee to run the company. Mergers don't like executive committees which tend to stop things happening rather than make things happen. Executives must do their jobs to be effective.

The major shift in this was that for the first time ICL, in conjunction with the British Government, wanted the entire Univac base in Europe and the Commonwealth brought in to the deal. The two exercises were quite different in Univac's mind and would require a very large cash injection. Nevertheless Univac did not reject the position and decided to study the inclusion of Europe, South Africa and Australia.

Discussions then took place with the senior Univac principals and their financial advisers. Univac questioned the feasibility of putting together this entire European operation. Univac's assets and profits in Europe were much larger than ICL's. One response was to pool the two companies. Pooling at that stage was popular – Dunlop Pirelli for instance had recently pooled.

The problems were severe management conflicts as someone had to be in charge. A fair amount of discussion took place to confirm the fact that the advisers realized that the assets and profits were disproportionately high in Univac *vis-à-vis* ICL but it was becoming clear there were other movements behind the scenes because Siemens had just announced their decision to merge their computer activities with the French company C2I. Indeed Phillips also joined in this consortium which was later to be called Unidata and clearly dialogue was taking place with the Europeans and ICL at the same time as the discussions were taking place between ICL and Univac. The idea of bringing the Americans into Europe in any way, shape or form clearly was anathema to continental Europeans and therefore you had in effect a triangular discussion process.

About this time it was important that I established the security of tenure of Tom Hudson and then tackled the Government, which said beyond doubt he would be there to stay. If we had done nothing else, we had at least secured Tom's continuing position in his job. So by mid-September we had reached a position where there was a feeling there was much to be gained by this merger between the two companies but personal interests and investment requirements were pulling in their own directions and therefore the cohesion of the debate was not going forward in an encouraging way, particularly bearing in mind that Univac had agreed to surrender its majority control in the UK to meet the requirements of ICL.

A great deal of study work then proceeded showing that the combination of Univac and ICL, calling the company Univac International Computers, could lead to a combined market share in Europe in excess of 50 per cent while IBM's market share would drop to about 30 per cent.

These were very encouraging figures and I agreed that work was undertaken to assess the role of asset funding of the companies. Univac were very sceptical about the ICL figures possibly because of poor profitability, and because one of the recommendations involved buying back Rental Assets. They believed the cash could be put to much better use than simply bolstering up the balance sheet to make the company look as if it was worth more.

Really what was coming through was, and particularly following a meeting in mid-September with the Government, that external opposition was developing to what was described as a sell-out to the Americans even though the Americans would take up a minority interest. On the other hand, they didn't particularly want to say this up front in case we ran away, not only in terms of the ICL deal but also because Univac's investment programme was important to the UK Government.

We were left with the distinct impression that the Government did want to sort out the ownership control issues at ICL, not simply for the prospects of a major merger with Univac but to merge ICL with the European companies.

In November the Government's position became clearer. They emphatically stated that they wanted ICL/Univac Europe with effective as well as real control in the UK. They did not see any possibility of cooperating with the French or the Germans and they were not prepared to reinforce Tom Hudson's position as Chairman of the company. They quite clearly at this stage had moved away from the European solution.

In the same month Univac agreed to accept the European ICL merger, sticking to their requirements of product control and management input, and had even got down details as to what size the companies were in different countries and what would be the combined value of the merger.

In December it was becoming clear that a political block was being put on this merger and a meeting at Secretary of State level attempted to placate Univac with the suggestion they would hope to keep Univac/ICL discussions going. In the event they weren't kept going and in April 1973 it was recognized by the Government that there was no further point in discussion. They subsequently thanked the various parties for their interest and left the discussions.

Like most things in life it emerged later on as to why these decisions were made. On 22 November the European Commission announced its broad programme proposals for encouraging the Community's own data processing industry and for promoting the effective use of its products. The Commission recommended further mergers in the industry and collaboration between member states. It admitted the company's products were unattractive to the market. It advocated joint financial arrangements on a limited number of development projects of an international character and stated that Europe could not afford to opt out of an industry of such social and political and economic importance. It failed to recognize the only European player viable was ICL who could not continue without major technological and marketing assistance.

It noted that despite the financial support and preferential policies of the French, British and German Governments the share in the world market of the four leading world companies, ICL, Siemens, CII and Phillips, was only 6 per cent and the regrouping of the industry was the only route to a big jump in relative size.

The Commission welcomed the formation of Unidata by Siemens, C2I and Philips and recommended member states should use public support in favour of the strongest possible industrial groupings, but it saw no immediate prospect of a combination of all leading companies given the existing plans of the two leading groups Unidata and ICL.

From then it was clear that the discussions taking place with Univac were also taking place between ICL and the other European companies and that the Commission was attempting to influence the total European merger of all European companies. It was quite clearly 'little Europe' thinking. In the words of Mr Christopher Leyton, the senior official concerned, 'The document does not say we would open up public markets to the exclusion of United States firms based in Europe. It does say that procurement policy should provide opportunities in the

European based industry and should seek to redress the competitive balance, i.e. the competitive balance against United States companies.'

Thinking there should be big development projects in such national fields as traffic control, environmental monitoring, meteorology, customs and trade statistics, I suggested that joint programmes or systems should be developed in such fields as social security and medical records.

Technical ability and collaboration and the development of a major computer force in Europe around ICL and Univac had been completely overlooked against a background of simple European political ideology. The plain fact of the matter is that whatever efforts were made to force ICL into a European consortium had actually stopped the industrial logical development of ICL and Univac merging.

Not long afterwards the collaboration between Philips, Siemens and C2I in the form of Unidata company broke up. ICL changed hands to Northern Electric, a Canadian company. The ICL product is heavily under the influence of Japanese technology, and the company finished up in Japanese ownership.

Univac subsequently emerged to make themselves a bigger and stronger force in the world, but none of them was able to improve its market position and play a role in the third generation of computer developments, namely in telecommunications and personal computing.

It seemed to me that the ICL/Univac activity particularly with the telecommunications input of Plessey and the design competence in GEC could have made Britain the most powerful, not just European, but international computing force. It seems our struggle with the European ideology is something we have been wrestling with for a long time and clearly in this case it did not help the technical or ideological development of the United Kingdom or Europe.

CHAPTER 4

Trucks and Buses

IN THE MIDDLE OF 1976 I began to question, particularly as I was spending so much time abroad, where my future lay. I had reached the rank of Vice-President of the Sperry Rand organization at a particularly young age and against the background that I was not a US citizen. Further progress to the Presidency and the Chairmanship, if achievable, could not happen without a change of nationality.

Secondly and probably more importantly, my daughters were now approaching their teens and I enjoyed their company and would like to spend more time with them if I could.

Whilst I did have ambition to be Chief Executive of a major organization it seemed natural, perhaps mistakenly, to me that it should be a British company. I was approached in the middle of 1976 and asked to consider taking on the vacant position of Managing Director of British Leyland Truck and Bus Division. This had become vacant as the Managing Director of some eight years experience, Ron Ellis, later to become Sir Ron Ellis, had taken up a position with the Ministry of Defence as Chief of Defence Sales.

I was initially approached by Alex Park, who was then the Chief Executive of British Leyland Motor Corporation, which had four divisions. The largest was cars, then truck and bus, followed by international, and finally special products – refrigeration and other forms of activity not normally associated with an automotive company. I found the discussion with Alex interesting and I was then interviewed by Sir Richard Dobson, known as Dicky Dobson, and Ian McGregor who was another member of the British Leyland Board. I liked them and I presume they liked me as shortly afterwards they offered the position which I took up on 1 October of that year.

I suppose of all the jobs I have held I often feel that the Truck and Bus job was really the most real. There is something rather powerful and grand, particularly about trucks, in the manufacture and testing and operation of them. Also the characteristics of the people that make trucks are very convincing

I don't think I was well received when I arrived at Leyland. There hadn't been many managing directors of Truck and Bus. Indeed apart from Ron Ellis, only two had held the position for many years and their portraits were painted and hung on the wall above my desk. I sometimes felt them stretching their hands out and touching me on the shoulder and saying, 'Don't do it that way, this is the way it has always been done.'

The first was Sir Edward Spurrer, after whom one of the main manufacturing plants was named and who in effect built up the business of Leyland Trucks and Leyland Buses. The second was Lord Stokes, who had bought a variety of companies and consolidated the UK truck market before going on to be the chairman of British Leyland Company itself. Don Stokes had bought companies like Guy, EEC, Scammell and eventually, when Leyland merged with the British Motor Corporation, their truck division also came to the company.

It was a big business and it was a big job. There were eleven plants and 35,000 people. During my first year of office the company produced its highest ever output of 65,000 vehicles and made its largest ever profit of close on £70 million.

It wasn't difficult to actually get the profit and output up. It was a question of breaking down the organization and appointing people with the sole responsibility to drive the production forward, making two or three key decisions to cure products to get the quality and output high, and then removing the biggest single onerous burden on the profit and loss account, namely the horrendous warranty costs.

An example of this was the so-called 500 engine. A nickname for the 500 engine was the 'headless monster'. Leyland had been at the forefront of engine design and pioneered the so-called turbo-charged engine which increases the pressure and combustion activities in the engine itself. The technical difficulty was that turbo-charging substantially increased the cylinder pressure and temperature. It was believed that the conventional engine gasket and removable top could not stand these pressure and temperature conditions.

They therefore designed an engine which was cast as a complete engine block with an integrated solid top. It was not a bad idea but there were serious difficulties with lubrication which meant that the engine would run excessively hot and so fail prematurely. In one third of the cases before it had reached its customer, in the second third of the cases before the truck was one year old.

Clearly these warranty items created a massive hole in the profits of the business. To me it was an easy decision, to the senior staff it was difficult. We had to take one step back to the old engine and end development and production of the new engine, which was never likely to work.

I suppose only a newcomer could have done that. What I am actually saying is that Leyland had to admit that it was no longer pre-eminent in engine design. We went back to an engine known as a 6.8 litre which Leyland had licensed to both SAAB and DAF and which was the backbone of their growing penetration of the European truck market.

A serious legal oversight was that a clause specifying that most of the benefits one gets from the licence, namely the improvements that the licensee develops, which are transferred back to the original owner of the engine, had been left out of the agreement. So the basic Leyland engine, which had served so well for so long, been improved by its competitors, and we had no value from that improvement.

It wasn't a technologically exciting step, but it was a serious and sensible business decision and turned the business into profitability in a very short period of time.

As I mentioned, the Leyland Truck and Bus business was a composition of a variety of acquisitions. It had over twenty truck types at that stage, all of different origin. A decision had been made to invest in new designs and new assemblies. So we set in motion three main programmes. First was the design and construction of the vehicle assembly hall which was a vast building, completed shortly before I left, which would have accommodated something in the region of twelve football pitches. It effectively halved the manpower and production time of the standard truck.

We set in train the construction of a large research and development site to assist the new product development.

The problem was that with so many different kinds of trucks how do you rationalize and develop a new line? What had been decided was that product effort and design should go into new 40-ton plus European trucks to compete in the European market, Leyland's penetration of which was relatively small. It didn't make sense to me. We needed a range of trucks almost on a building block basis, with a small number of bodies or cabs and a small number of power trains. The power train is the combination of the engine, gearbox and axle.

The concept study justified the proposal to use three cabs and four power trains to completely replace the entire existing truck line. That was designated the T45 line and I guess if I achieved anything it was getting it actually on the road. Today of course the T45 and its successor are the principal products from the Leyland operation.

It was interesting seeing the wood mock-ups being built and the early prototypes put together and driving them on the test track. Indeed you could see a very interesting future with Leyland involving some very difficult decisions such as planned closures and staff reductions in a rather hostile but nevertheless manageable labour employment environment. Whilst the recipe was not acceptable to the strong unions it was recognized by them that it was necessary for the long term success and indeed survival of the truck and bus business.

There were, however, two major setbacks in that period and one lack of moral support for a major strategic move, not unlike the ICL drama, which I will call the Fiat drama and come back to at a later stage.

Leyland, as I mentioned, was shipping 65,000 vehicles at that stage of which half were going to overseas countries, in particular Commonwealth countries. They were what we called normal control trucks; in other words they had bonnets like the old trucks had and operated well in difficult terrain, particularly in Africa.

On 19 May 1977 a leading daily newspaper ran a front page and four or five other pages with a lead story alleging corruption at Leyland Truck and Bus. Indeed it specified a particular number of corrupt acts which it intended to run in detail the following day. This was banner headline material and indeed the contracts in the countries that were mentioned were authentic and did exist. What was also shown the following day was a series of letters allegedly from the then Secretary of State for Trade Mr Eric Varley to Lord Ryder, Chairman of the National Enterprise Board and Leyland's principal shareholder; there was also a letter from Lord Ryder to a few executives in Leyland. I, while not named, was the executive to whom the correspondence was addressed.

It was immediately clear from the main story on the 19th that the letters were forgeries, even by looking at them in the newspaper, and that the countries and accounts mentioned were referring to the normal commission arrangements that applied to selling trucks abroad. Normal commission discount on standard list price would be in the region of 20 per cent in order that the distributor could recoup his costs of service and make a reasonable return for his effort. These numbers had been listed against the accounts during an examination by an internal auditor called Barton. Barton, for his part, had given them to a third party who had doctored them to appear to be inducements and bribes, as opposed to commission, and the newspaper had been wrongfully and deliberately misled by this false information.

After urgent discussions, on Saturday the newspaper ran a full front page retraction, in particular pointing out the errors in the allegations that they had made in the previous two days. You may well say that that was sufficient and that it was a very satisfactory thing for them to do, but the damage it did to Leyland was irretrievable.

The allegations appeared in over 100 foreign newspapers and probably had 1,000 column metres of print. The retraction on the Saturday appeared in few and had only 1 per cent equivalent in terms of print. In some countries the purchasing authorities were in fear of their life at some of the second-hand allegations they heard. The export business of Leyland Truck and Bus to its traditional markets collapsed. The culprits who perpetrated this fraud against the newspaper were subsequently tried in a criminal court.

The second substantial change was that of the Chairman of British Leyland, on whose Board it had been a pleasure to serve. Dickie Dobson was a most likable and accomplished man who had for many years been the Chairman of British American Tobacco before succeeding the previous Chairman of Leyland who died in office after only a short period of time. Dickie had a standard set of jokes but in terms of political correctness some may not have conformed to the standards, whatever they are, that the left and liberals demand. Regrettably, on one occasion during an afternoon lunch speech he used a number of these jokes which caused a furore as they involved jokes about 'wogs' and overseas ethnic groups, and he felt it was wise to resign.

This was a sad loss to the Company which was struggling with massive industrial problems particularly on the car side, and was con-stantly under attack by the unions. These, it should be remembered, were the dying years or even the dying days of the Callaghan Labour Government. The main problems were universal strikes throughout the country and the Government's inability to influence these strikes, which were principally in the public sector, the nationalized industries being a main part of that.

Leyland was not actually in the public sector. Ten per cent of equity was still quoted on the stock market, so it did not have the same degree of protection of being owned by the Government, that many of the nationalized industries had. The NEB had at this stage also changed its chairman to Mr Leslie Murphy and he decided to pick the next chairman of British Leyland, Michael Edwardes, subsequently Sir Michael. It was an intriguing choice because Michael had limited industrial experience on the scale required for this kind of operation and had some unusual techniques in choosing executives, based on psychological tests. One couldn't help but feel that the decision was a political one. The Labour Government had to tackle these constant strikes. The only really large organization which wasn't backed by the Government, but was seen to be a Government agency, was British Leyland and I believe the Government of the day needed what they thought was a strong, able, determined man to take on the unions. Frankly there wasn't any question that this was exactly what Michael Edwardes was and indeed that is exactly what he did.

But that type of approach to management is not conducive to balance sheet wealth generation and industrial growth.

One of Michael's first actions was to decide to close a production plant. I think this was the right and proper course of action. But he chose, I believe perhaps for emotional reasons, to close the wrong plant.

The day he joined, the Liverpool No. 2 plant, which was a new assembly plant for the Triumph TR7, had gone on strike. They had never been on strike before. Productivity was low particularly comparing it to the Ford Halewood plant only a few miles away where productivity was double and strikes were unheard of. In part this was due to the practice of putting Birmingham management in charge of Scousers. Strangely enough German management in charge of Scousers worked at Halewood, but Birmingham management in charge of Scousers did not work in the Leyland plant in Liverpool. So the inability to grow in-house management to run the plant was the principal reason for its poor performance.

I was against closing Liverpool for several reasons: that I lived there and could almost see the plant from my house and I knew the people; that I believed it could be improved and managed more effectively given the example of Ford Halewood; and that the knock-on effect of taking the assembly of the TR7 elsewhere increased its costs in such a way as to be detrimental to Leyland sports car market share.

There were two areas in which Leyland cars were successful in that period. One was sports cars, in which probably in terms of variety and choice it was the world leader; and the other was the Mini which I'll come to in a minute.

Anyway my voice was not heard in this situation, the plant was closed and consequently the Leyland share of the sports car market started to fall quite rapidly.

The second decision which I found difficult to understand was to switch from the Mini replacement. This was the largest volume car that Leyland made and indeed served a part of the market that few other car manufacturers catered for, to the new Metro which instead of being a single person's car like the Mini was in fact a small family car and subsequently suffered competition from all the major European rivals already well established.

The Mini's replacement, the so-called ADO 88, was at this stage quite advanced, so starting all over again with the Metro meant lost years in sales of the Mini replacement. Again that decision was made and again its effect was I think to lose Leyland the chance of staying in the volume car market at the lower end.

The Company was building 1.2 million cars at that stage. As we all know the figures are now substantially lower.

Michael Edwardes took all but one of the executive directors off the main Board. This naturally caused personal resentment. I am sure I felt it and may well have showed it. It is sometimes said that he and I had fallen out. I don't think that was the case. I think we had our own ways of doing things and I respected the manner in which he conducted himself and explained himself and made difficult decisions on the basis of authority and responsibility. But I do say again he was running the business to solve the Union problem, whereas I had always been used to running a business to increase its balance sheet strength.

So in a sense my leaving was almost inevitable. I think if there was one reason that caused me to resign it was the failure of a very important corporate restructuring in the truck industry, of which Leyland could be an integral part.

The position of this was that very shortly after joining Leyland I met Engineer Baccarria, my equivalent running the Fiat truck organization in Italy. Most truck companies had rationalized. Mercedes was dominant, Fiat was No. 2 and most of the other companies had co-operative arrangements. Leyland from a European standpoint had become isolated.

We had a variety of discussions with International Harvester who owned DAF, with Renault, particularly on vans, with Scania who were a very efficient and effective company and with Volvo. None of these, with the exception of the Renault Company, were terribly serious; it was getting to know each other. But with Fiat we did have numerous meetings and discussions, the whole tenor of which was that Fiat wanted a transfer of the truck manufacturing centre from Italy to the UK. They did want to merge Fiat and Leyland Trucks and they did want Leyland Trucks to be the principal shareholder in this new European arrangement.

We discussed rationalization of the product, the European marketing and the construction of the Board and I had been progressing these discussions quite well during the tenure of Dickie Dobson's chairmanship. But on Edwardes's arrival, with the general turmoil arising from the changes he naturally wanted to make and I think based on advice, they were very much sidelined.

It is difficult for me to say why but there was a feeling somewhere at the Chairman's level, or perhaps at Government level, that it was not a good idea for a British company to merge with an Italian company. It may well have been that other arrangements, such as that with Dunlop Pirelli, had not worked well and the whole idea of pooling and merging had become an unpopular concept.

I do feel, and I did feel then, that the only way forward for a company of that scale and size was in the European dimension and yet again, I suspect, another opportunity was lost to build a sound industry run from and owned by Britain.

What happened to Leyland of course is now history. Its bus operations, which were fundamentally successful because it had almost 100 per cent of the double-decker bus market and a very high proportion of the single-decker market, fell away for the very simple reason that double-decker buses were no longer built. Indeed the only other place that they were built was Hong Kong. That business subsequently sold for a few million pounds to its management, who in a year sold it for £30 million or so to one of the Scandinavian companies.

The truck business was sold to DAF in Holland, who subsequently went into liquidation. Leyland Trucks became the object of a management buy-out, working a very efficient and effective operation based on the Leyland assembly plant, producing something between 10 and 20 per cent of the trucks that the Leyland Truck company used to produce and marketing these trucks through a DAF marketing organization. It was then bought by an American truck manufacturer.

The fiascoes of the year, probably the best way to describe them, were the Annual General Meetings at which a large number of small shareholders would turn up and create a rumpus. The general tenor of their attack was that the management was no good and this was the place to exercise their opinions. These meetings could go on for a long time, sometimes leading to a vote which was rather fatuous when 90 per cent of the voting power was in the hands of the chairman who held the proxy for the principal owner, National Enterprise Board.

On one occasion of great disorder, members of the AGM decided to speak in German and on being asked to speak in English pointed out that there was nothing in the Articles of the Company that required people to speak in English, and indeed there wasn't. But you can well imagine the mayhem that all this commotion caused.

But interestingly enough there was a Mr Faulkner, who on my election to the Board at the first AGM I attended, stood up and proposed himself as an independent member of the Board. This proposition of course was rejected because as the Chairman pointed out he had failed to follow procedure and in any event the Chairman had 90 per cent of the voting power.

Mr Faulkner has become a national figure in standing up to nominate himself for Board membership on various large company boards. Strangely enough, although he may not have realized it, he figured again in a quite important moment in my future, when I was first being elected to another Board. At that stage he wasn't actually proposing himself as a Director, but he was making a point.

Some of the interesting people I met included Harold Musgrave. I had made him Managing Director of the Leyland complex. Harold was a tenacious individual who served his apprenticeship together with Red Robbo, the Union leader down at Longbridge. Harold was to go on to become a Managing Director of Leyland Cars and indeed it was he who ultimately faced the battle with Red Robbo which finally broke the back of Union power inside the Longbridge plant of Leyland Cars. I sometimes feel he never really got the recognition for it, maybe because he was rather outspoken and indifferent to authority and was very much inclined to present his own opinion regardless of the sensitivity that others might have. He is now in semi-retirement and was president of Aston Villa Football Club, so we do from time to time have the chance to meet.

Another interesting man was Sir David Plaistow, who was at that stage the Managing Director of Rolls-Royce Motors. David had a very smooth and pleasant manner, which made him an ideal man to lead Rolls-Royce Motors. Leyland's connection with them was Pressed Steel, the Leyland subsidiary that made the car bodies, and Truck and Bus cast the engine blocks for the engines. On the other hand Rolls Royce also made large engines which they called the Eagle Engines and approached the company to put them into the Leyland trucks. Some progress was made on that.

David subsequently went on to merge Rolls-Royce with Vickers, and be Chief Executive and Chairman of Vickers Company. We have kept in touch on a casual golfing relationship since.

Gerald Ronson was one of the large Leyland Truck distributors through his company Heron. He was a good businessman to deal with, straightforward, down to earth. Also worthy of note was the Bamford family of J.C. Bamford, a very successful excavating company before the closure of the Bathgate Works in Scotland, who at that time equipped most of their excavators with Leyland engines.

One of my last visits while I was in Leyland Truck and Bus was to Iran, shortly before the revolution of 1979. I visited Tehran, Shiriz and Isfahan. Iran at that stage was taking between 2,000 and 5,000 vehicles a year from Leyland Truck and Bus but this stopped after the revolution. The Scammell business had built a very large tank transporter for which we had high hopes for a big order. Iran needed to move its tanks great distances along its various borders and tanks have to be moved on transporters as opposed to under their own power.

It was a frightening experience being in Iran, particularly in Shiriz and Isfahan with their great rows of helicopters and planes at the airports. One was shepherded off the plane into the airport lounges in case you were observing the military strength of the country. At Isfahan in the Shab-abbas Hotel, we were infested by cockroaches. I was infected by what I think was one of the worst stomach disorders that I have personally experienced, which left me completely shattered and physically exhausted.

On the last day the Mayor of Isfahan, Shahastani, invited us and other people to a cocktail party at his home, which was virtually a fortress surrounded by people with machine-guns. I am told, although it may well have been a fable, that his escape helicopter was under the swimming pool. Quite how it would be removed to fly from under the swimming pool I don't know, but it does illustrate the tremendous sense of anxiety that existed in Iran immediately before the revolution.

The Queen at Leyland, 1977.

My very last meeting at Leyland Truck and Bus was with Ian McGregor, in New York as it happened, when I had flown to International Harvester to advise them that I was passing the job on to somebody else. Ian regretted that I had made the decision to go but we kept in touch on a number of occasions subsequently.

CHAPTER 5

Telecommunications

Having left Leyland Truck and Bus I had recently re-married and I thought a break of some kind would be useful. But a number of people made approaches to see if I had an interest. One in particular was the Chairman of EMI, Sir John Reed, who discussed the situation facing his company and the need for a Chief Executive.

It is hard to imagine anybody intellectually more honest than Sir John. He portrayed without hesitation the real problems facing the Company, the principal one being the difficulties of the scanner. EMI had led the field, but the Americans had come back with a better and highly competitive product and creating what appeared to be potentially very serious financial problems for the EMI company.

The other was Parry Rogers, the Personnel Director of Plessey, who kept in touch and clearly wanted me to consider a position at Plessey.

Before I got down to that I seemed to be meeting old friends. I mentioned that Ian McGregor turned up. So did Tom Hudson, John

Butler, a colleague at Sperry, and Sir Peter Thompson who was the chairman of National Freight Corporation making his reputation on the privatization of the National Freight Corporation.

So I had for perhaps the only time in my career a couple of months to spend simply meeting people and renewing old acquaintanceships. I met Sir John Clark and Michael Clark and the new Finance Director of Plessey, Peter Marshall, and as is the way with Plessey, it sometimes takes them a little while to make up their mind. But the job they were really asking me to take was the Managing Director of their Telecommunications and Office Systems, which was really the guts and soul of the Plessey company. It had been its big profit earner and was running into huge losses, damaging the performance of the whole Company.

The man who held the job was a Dr Bill Willetts and I was somewhat puzzled, and so were others, as to why he was prepared to take a somewhat backstage role in this job which he had held so covetously for about ten years. The reason subsequently became clear. Shortly after I joined Plessey Dr Willetts left to become the Chief Executive of Vickers. In physical terms it was not much of a move because his office at Plessey was on the 21st floor of Millbank Tower and at Vickers on the 27th floor.

I planned not to start at Plessey until 1 October 1978 in order to have a rest, but that wasn't to be. John Clarke, being the man that he is, ferrets at things once he gets his mind to it and was constantly pushing me to be involved before I officially joined. So by the time I actually joined Plessey I had been to numerous meetings and met all the executives who would be my team, so I was able to get off to a reasonable flying start.

I think it is worth while looking at the situation appertaining to the telecommunications industry at that time. There were two major changes taking place. One was that telecommunications equipment had always been electrical/mechanical, lots of chattering relays, very manpower intensive in manufacturing and maintenance. It had now become electronic; even worse than that it had become computer driven or even totally computerized. The facilities that the system offered were far better and, more particularly, the size of the telephone exchanges were reduced to one tenth. This had serious manpower consequences for the manufacturing volume and maintenance requirements.

The second situation was that in any event Plessey's main customer was the then Post Office. Some years earlier the Conservative Government had reduced Government expenditure which was almost entirely passed on to manufacturing activities. This had led to a 60 per cent overnight cut in the orders for the obsolescent exchanges.

The management responded to this by cut-throat competition, and under-priced their products. This meant that the more equipment they made, the more money they lost. As with most activities in the late 1970s, strikes were constant and in particular in the Liverpool factories, especially the big one at Edge Lane. As every department was inter-linked through the process of production, almost invariably someone was arguing over piecework rates and there were constant disruptions and frequent strikes.

This obviously could not carry on. The Plessey Board's answer to it was to close the Liverpool factory down. So there I was again arriving on a site not far from home employing 12,000 people, about to be closed down for the simple reason that the Company had been unable to manage the work force.

It had a familiar ring. I had lost the battle for the Liverpool factory at Leyland but I did not want to lose this one. This was an easier one to win because in reality the Plessey Company could not close the Liverpool factory down without serious financial damage to the company. The sheer cost of it was so prohibitive that they just could not afford anything other than an organized reduction and certainly couldn't contemplate an overnight exit.

I made this point to the Board and the Board accepted it, with great reluctance but they wanted to know how it was going to be cured. It was solved in the traditional way by appointing good management which existed in the company but was not in Liverpool. My first appointment was somebody with whom I was going to have a close association for some years, Eric Clark, based at Poole, whose principal business was the traffic and data systems. I asked him to become the Chief Executive of the main exchange business which was based at Edge Lane, Liverpool.

So by and large there already was there, but not necessarily in the right places, an effective management team.

I had an office at Liverpool but eventually moved to London because the normal demands of the job kept me in London most of the time. I maintained a home in the North because that was really where I thought I belonged.

On my first day at Plessey I walked into a situation where I could not go into my office. This was because the latest innovative strike idea had been a management lock-out. In other words the workers refused to allow the management into the plant, or any plant, and carried on with production. This was a short lived exercise for a variety of reasons. Whatever the general view of management is, if they are not there to administrate it doesn't take long before a business ceases to function. We were let back in, so to speak, and I was confronted with a cheque to sign for two weeks' wages for the workers who had worked without any management presence. I refused to sign this cheque on the grounds that unless the management knew who was in they couldn't pay anybody because this might result in people being paid who hadn't actually worked.

This caused friction and another mass meeting, attended by my brother, who worked in the plant and was horrified at the prospect of me being the Managing Director of the group. The shop stewards were ridiculed for suggesting another management lock-out. The operatives had formed the view that this management rather liked the idea of management being locked out in order to get production at no cost. At any rate, everybody went back to work and another strike action started. It involved the testers in certain sections who would have selective strikes, which resulted in a handful of people stopping the whole production.

The only course of action left open to me was to lay off every person in the Union, which was ASTMS Union. This led to ASTMS's strike. ASTMS paid their people the highest strike pay of any union and did not want a prolonged strike of 600 people. The executive of ASTMS were desperate for people to return to work. Their representatives came to the site and put pressure on them to get back to work again, which they did.

This wasn't a very enjoyable six months, as you can well imagine, trying to get the business to function properly. However, what we had done during that period was to lay down a plan for the Edge Lane factory involving a reduction in the work force to below 3,000, additionally putting in substantial investment to ensure employment for about one third of the people and at least putting the rest in a position where they knew where they stood.

Brian Redhead put together a presentation of that programme. He was telling employees what the future was, where they were positioned in the future, and what the management was trying to do to save the factory and build the business. We didn't have another strike after that, which was a most interesting result. If you tell people what the company future is, as best you can, with some substance, then you get their co-operation and people start working for the interest of the long term survival and success of the organization.

At that time a system known as TXE4 and TXE4A had been developed for STC (Standard Telephone Cables), and was shared equally amongst three major telecommunications manufacturers – ourselves, STC and GEC. GEC and Plessey were making the equipment under licence. It was like most other orders of its type from the British Post Office, as it then was. It was based on a cost plus formula, which was totally unsatisfactory from a whole variety of standpoints. There was no incentive for the designers or manufacturers or anybody else to make it cheaper. The more expensive it was the higher the profit that the company made. It tied management's hands in terms of managing resources and improving efficiency.

One evening Sir William Barlow, who was then Chairman, together with my STC and GEC counterparts, had dinner with us. This we would do on a monthly basis. I proposed that if we were to freeze the prices at the 1979 level, and have no further inspections and cost plus formulae for a five year period, it would be far more effective and far more efficient. My proposal was made against the background of the sheer size of the capital expenditure that we were putting in, and additionally the co-operative way in which the Post Office, Plessey, STC and GEC were all working together to develop the new System X, which I will come to later.

Sir William grabbed this opportunity, although my other two colleagues were less than enthusiastic. This led to a substantial reduction in manufacturing costs and improved efficiency and was one of the principal drivers for the rapid increase in profitability of the Plessey company.

When I joined Plessey in 1978, the Company's financial performance was poor. At about the same time a new Finance Director, Peter Marshall, was appointed. Peter and I had an excellent working relationship. Profits were around £40 million, the greater proportion of which came from the 17.5 per cent ICL investment to which I referred earlier, although the investment was not accompanied by a cash inflow as ICL paid a lower percentage dividend than Plessey did. So the profits, flattered by the ICL interest, placed a heavier burden on the Plessey cash flow in terms of funding its dividends.

Shares were around 36p and within days of my joining Sir John and Michael Clark sold the majority of their remaining holding in the Plessey company. This did not give Peter and me very much encouragement, particularly as the company was very vulnerable to take-over by three or four other electronics companies of the time such as Racal and GEC, who were doing extremely well.

Peter Marshall set about the Plessey Company corporate restructure which involved the sale of many non-relevant businesses who were making either losses or poor returns. In particular the sale of ICL shareholding brought a large cash injection into Plessey and removed the dividend liability to which I referred.

I tackled the reorganization of the major manufacturing plants, also overseeing the product development activities for System X and the development of small office systems based on a product called IDX, which was a computer based telephone exchange capable of many office functions, and was at that stage beginning to take the lead in Britain as the major office exchange.

We had set about modernizing the Edge Lane plant, which gave some satisfaction to the employees there that the management meant what it said, but the overwhelming problem facing us was the need to complete the development and tooling of System X which was the new computerized telephone exchange. This would replace every telephone exchange in England and would be more effective, cheaper and faster, being a fully digital system.

I will discuss at some length the way that the System X organizational problems, or even possibly the political problems, were resolved in the late 1970s and early 1980s, during which time the British Post Office was split up into British Telecom and the Post Office itself. Sir William Barlow left and Sir George Jefferson (known to his friends and colleagues as Jeff) became the first chairman of BT prior to and after its privatization.

System X was organized on a four party basis: BT, STC, GEC and Plessey. From the Managing Directors Committee down through all the different processes of the research and development programme there were four parties present, so instead of having one piece of paper it would become four pieces of paper. By the time it got to the R & D level it could be sixteen or a multiple of that pieces of paper, together with all the administration and people that went with it.

Quite apart from the cost of all that, the confusion was immense and it is clear that a great deal of money was being spent with insufficient output, and time scales were not being met because of the administrative burden imposed by the organization. Additionally too, we attempted to compete with the French and the Germans to sell main exchange equipment abroad. To do that we had to form a company called BTS (British Telecommunications Systems) and a voice from the past emerged in the form of Chris Chataway as its non-Executive Chairman and John Sharpley, an executive from Plessey, went to be its Managing Director.

They had the doubtful task of representing four points of view wherever they went. It was hardly an appropriate organization to impress prospective overseas buyers, particularly as the product didn't exist and was only in test form.

This situation continued for some time and Plessey set about trying to convince the Government that the responsibility for System X development, and hopefully the production, should rest with one manufacturer, which not surprisingly it believed should be Plessey. In other words there should be some form of competition for System X design and production. This was an interesting exercise as it was somewhat like the ICL/Univac proposed merger. It involved competition between STC, GEC and Plessey, the support of BT and the Government endorsement. BT was still a nationalized industry.

Much of the initial consideration of this was made by the Minister for Industry, Adam Butler, subsequently Sir Adam Butler, who paid a visit to Liverpool in September 1980 to try to get an appreciation of what was involved in the design and manufacture of System X.

It was further discussed the same month with Jeff Jefferson, the new Chairman, and Peter Benton, the Managing Director of British Telecom, pushing the obvious advantages of one company designing and producing System X, but clearly we had a vested interest in this and they listened but gave no reaction.

The following year, quite early on, John Clark, Jeff Jefferson and I pursued the idea, over lunch, with Peter Carry, who was the Permanent Secretary at the Department of Trade and Industry, and Ray Croft who was a senior Civil Servant, and the idea was mooted with Kenneth Baker, who had become the Minister for Information Technology, and met with Sir John and myself. It is interesting that during this period, as the profits were beginning to come through, Plessey shares rose quite substantially, and indeed peaked at 730p, i.e. twenty times what they were in 1978. We became a very much watched share by the market.

Managing Directors, System X. Author, Plessey; John Whyte, Chief Examiner, BT; Geoff Samsun, STC.

They frequently called upon me to try to glean from me what was happening with regard to System X. Clearly they didn't get told, because apart from anything else we didn't know, we simply had a scheme of thinking involving modernized manufacturing techniques, part of which were now installed in Liverpool, and we believed that we had the main competence of technical know-how in the development of System X.

In August of the same year, 1981, Sir George Jefferson came to see System X in some detail, again at Liverpool, together with John Whyte, his Chief Engineer, who was convinced of the need to rationalize manufacture. Ray Atkinson another senior civil servant who retired to the north-east of England, was also very active in the assessment of the costs and benefits of rationalization of product development and manufacturing.

Through that year a variety of meetings took place. Adam Butler,

John Clark and I met in October. The issue rumbled on into 1982 and more important meetings, not the least of which was prompted by the decision of Patrick Jenkin, the Secretary of State for Industry, to visit all the companies and form his own personal view, which of the three could take on the prime responsibility. There was a big prize to be won for this one. The modernization programme of BT was running at £2000 million per annum at that stage and a very large part of it was, and would be, the replacement of all the existing electro-mechanical exchanges by System X exchanges. With years of guaranteed work and profits as a consequence of winning this prize it was one to fight for and we persisted with our intention to capture the prize itself, rather than settling for a sharing basis, which would have been inefficient.

Round about this time, I am not quite sure exactly when, Kenneth Baker sent for me and my counterparts in GEC and STC and said the Government was really dissatisfied with the progress of System X and the cost involved, and he wanted us individually or collectively, however we saw fit, to place a proposition before him as to how the difficulties could be overcome and the cost reduced.

It wasn't difficult for us of course – we had been working on it for the last two years. The other two were less keen, certainly GEC. STC, who had the biggest part of the TXE4 programme, weren't in any event keen on the simple electronic exchanges being replaced by the computerised System X exchange.

I rang Kenneth Baker a week later and said we were ready to put our proposal before him. I admired him – he said he would make himself available twenty-four hours a day to receive these proposals, and he was somewhat bemused by our rapid response to his request. Our proposal was of course to take over all responsibility for the R & D programme for the international marketing and for the sole manufacturing. We never believed we would actually get this, but that's what we actually placed before him and the output benefits in cost and accelerated time scale were well argued in our paper.

The issue was not reaching any conclusion. I think that various other companies were making an input, I don't know what, but decisions certainly seemed to be slow in forthcoming, when we decided after much soul searching inside Plessey, to buy Stromberg-Carlson, the only independent US main telephone exchange manufacturer. The rest was made by AT&T or by GTE, the second largest provider of telecommunications services in the States.

General Dynamic Corporation wanted to divest themselves of anything that wasn't purely military, being themselves the manufacturers of the F15 and F16 fighters and nuclear submarines, not to mention Cruise missiles and other similar military apparatus.

By an amazing coincidence Wynne Wells, who was the finance director of General Dynamics, had been a colleague of mine back in my computer days and that facilitated an easy discussion. The delay in the acquisition of Stromberg-Carlson was a natural reluctance by Plessey to invest in America after an early acquisition had proved financially unsatisfactory.

John Whyte, the Chief Engineer of BT, was taken to Stromberg-Carlson to see the activity out there and, incidentally, we acquired the business the same day the Epcot Centre was opened, so it was easy to remember the precise day that the business was handed over to us.

I think really it must have been the brave decision to buy Stromberg-Carlson that finally turned the balance of the consideration in our favour regarding System X. Plessey was designated the main development contractor with prime responsibility for the completion of the development of System X, with prime responsibility to give to GEC one third of the development work on a sub-contract basis during the early manufacturing period.

Plessey and GEC were designated as the two manufacturing companies who would from time to time share the work and then would compete with each other on an ongoing basis. STC was withdrawn completely from the whole System X programme, which really meant the end of their days in main telephone exchange manufacturing. British Telecommunications Systems Company, chaired by Chris Chataway and run by John Sharpley to export System X, was closed down and the export responsibilities were then left with Plessey and GEC to compete wherever and on whatever basis they wished.

It was a huge Government decision, a major rationalization, which did not please Lord Weinstock and led to acrimonious statements, but in the end I am sure it was the right one in terms of modernizing the British Telecommunications network, which today is one of the most up to date in the world. It was certainly good for Liverpool Edge Lane, which is now the most modern telecommunications manufacturing plant in Europe and gives no trouble in terms of industrial relationships. It was a nice one to win and a very satisfying experience.

All this led to the usual involvement. Commissioner D'Avignon, who was the Commissioner for Industry in Europe, invited me to join his European industrial strategic group with the intent to grow a strong telecommunications and computing industry. There was theoretical discussion and value in the personal contacts of my counterparts from the other countries. There were invitations from Phillips to examine their telecommunications business and look for areas of co-operation, and likewise strong interest by Siemens to see if there was a possible association, which ultimately, after my day, materialized between Plessey Telecommunications and Siemens themselves.

On the office equipment side the hub of the whole activity was the integrated digital exchange that I mentioned previously. A smaller version of this was made and sold in great numbers through British Telecomms. Inter-active terminals operating on the telephone exchange provided much additional functionality in terms of transfer switching and other now quite popular facilities on telephone exchanges were developed.

We clearly weren't going to make an integrated office system by ourselves, and we sought, through long discussions with Burroughs, a co-operative arrangement between the two companies. We would have got somewhere had Burroughs not decided to merge with Univac, create Unysis and form an enlarged US operating computer company.

It's a strange life. You keep on meeting the same people over and over in different circumstances, even at an international level.

As well as IDX Plessey made a lot of progress in the field of the facsimile machine and was in fact leading the field in terms of fax installations which were then somewhat slow and expensive, but technology and techniques were improving at a considerable rate.

The one area that we missed out on even though we worked on it was the cellular telephone. Unlike Racal we failed to enter the first bid and consequently we never took part in that very important developing part of British Telecommunications.

The associated activity during this later period of my stint with Plessey was to be elected the President of TEMA (Telecommunications Equipment Manufacturers Association). It was an interesting time to be President because whilst BT was the biggest customer it was also to be the biggest competitor. BT had been corporatized in preparation for privatization and a good many arguments were taking place as to who should operate in what markets.

There were some very interesting discussions which actually freed up the markets, unquestionably to BT's advantage, as their sheer financial clout somewhat helped their decision to buy Mitel which was a small Canadian telecommunications manufacturer that had a very good product.

But in the end BT failed to exploit this to put them in the position of manufacturer as well as service provider in the liberalized telecommunications market. One of my tasks was to lead an official trade mission to Tokyo and meet the major Japanese manufacturers where we were handsomely entertained, and also meet MITI (The Ministry for Industry and Trade). The Japanese were wholehearted in their advice and hospitality. We visited Jujitsu, NEC, Sharp, Oki, and Maribeni, the finance house. Sharp particularly impressed me when discussing long term plans. The President of Sharp simply said, 'If you can use it on a desk we make it, whether it is a pen or a computer.' This very simple philosophy showed right through the entire product line and quite clearly was a key factor in their worldwide success.

Another activity that we attempted to develop was one of cable and satellite transmission reception. This was a difficult subject in England because of the regulatory framework involving franchises on limited areas and taxation arrangements on capital expenditure. Some of this is now bearing fruit, but it did not develop at the rate the industry wanted.

We did however form a joint company with Scientific Atlanta who were one of the major companies in the States developing and manufacturing transmission and reception equipment for satellites. It was a useful exercise but did involve a fair amount of travel between the two locations to get the business going.

In 1983 it was now becoming apparent that my second marriage had major difficulties. A proposal was made to me to become Chief Executive at Littlewoods. This seemed to me to be a possibility to establish my family in the North West with two boys now of school age. In the event it failed. Although I had taken the job my wife wouldn't move from the south-east. My final parting activity was to speak at the Geneva Conference on Worldwide Telecommunications.

One aspect of the liberalization of the Plessey products is that I met many of the retailers with whom we were trying to sell telecommunications products. It was very demanding and hard work. I did enjoy my stay with Plessey. It was exciting to be in the forefront of technology again as I had been at Sperry. I met very many people politically and also internationally. To see the completion of the System X development programme and the milestone that it was in British Telecommunications was a very satisfying experience.

So with mixed feelings I moved on to my next assignment, namely Chief Executive of the Littlewoods Organization.

CHAPTER 6

Retail – Littlewoods

I WAS APPROACHED in early 1983 by Mr John Clement, who was then the recently appointed non-Executive Chairman of the Littlewoods Organization. Over a period of months, discussions took place with him on the basis that I be appointed Littlewoods first Group Chief Executive. Previously the company had always had a member of the Moores family as its full-time executive chairman.

I met the five shareholder directors in June 1983 and accepted their offer to join the company at the beginning of December. I visited the company on 11 November that year and met the senior staff, and took up my position on a full-time basis at the end of that month.

On 1 December I took up my appointment as the Chief Executive of the Littlewoods organization, and apart from the courtesy of Sir John, the Founder and President wishing to welcome me to the company, I decided I'd better spend some time with him before I

ventured out to meet with the rest of the organization. In that meeting
Sir John established an on-going dialogue regarding his concerns and
interests about Everton Football Club and football in general. It
became a regular discussion topic of ours in the years that followed,
over and above my briefing of him for the monthly board meetings
and giving him an overall view of the state of the business. We had
been in conversation for about two hours when I thought it was
probably time for me to go and meet the rest of the senior staff.
However I took the opportunity to ask Sir John for simply one word
of advice. He'd built that company and had run it all his life, and who
could give me a better pointer as to how to take the business forward
than him. He took this question with great suspicion and was reluctant
to carry on the conversation. He said, 'We'll put that to one side for a
moment.'

So we carried on talking about football and matters in general, and
then he said, 'I've only got one word of advice to you.' Mr John, as he
was known in the company, said, 'I have been through no end of
different circumstances with the same problems in this company. On
some occasions I've wanted to resolve it that way, or another way, or a
different way, or a new way, and on some occasions I've even
contradicted what I said previously quite simply because circumstances
had changed and the problem, whilst it might be the same, needed a
different resolution.' He added, 'The trouble with the people in the
company is that all, without exception, remember when I said, "Don't
do this, or don't do that," even though the context today or in the
future is quite different. That's always a reason for not doing things and
they will say to you, "Mr John doesn't like that, I know because he said
so." That is the biggest difficulty you're up against.'

I said, 'Not really, because if I wanted to do something I would insist
on it being done, and the very first person who says, "Mr John doesn't
like that," I will bring him in here to see you and you will back me to
the hilt, regardless of what it is I want to get done.'

His response to this was very guarded indeed and it really was, in a
sense, a pivotal point in our relationship because he concluded by

saying, 'I suppose really if I don't back you there's no prospect of you running this company. But for goodness sake, whoever it is you bring in, make sure it is not an issue that will be embarrassing for the two of us.'

I then went out to join the meeting and within five minutes one of the senior directors said, 'Oh, you can't do that, Mr John doesn't like it,' so I asked him to retire from the room with me to go and see Mr John. Before we even got through the door of the office, Mr John said, 'I told you somebody'd say it; I knew it would be that fool. If you're going to sack him it's the best thing you could do on your first day in office.'

I didn't sack the executive concerned, but word got round the company and from that day forwards my authority was accepted. Later on I may have been challenged by new people joining the company who thought they knew a better way of doing things as I was, in their eyes, one of the old guard.

The Company, as far as the Executives were concerned, was never a comfortable environment. I shall elaborate on this in a separate chapter. But by the fact of the family ownership or possibly as a reaction to it, the atmosphere was always one of suspicion and mistrust.

One of the first tasks I was asked to undertake was to investigate allegations against a previous Managing Director. Peter Moores asked me to do this and said he was acting on behalf of his father, Sir John. He suggested that the individual had been involved in unexplained practices when he was Chief Buyer at Littlewoods.

This person had been with Littlewoods for thirty-nine years and had ascended through the ranks to the position of Managing Director. The principal source of the allegations was a distant relative, who was, so to speak, on the wrong side of the family. In the early years Sir John, when he had some financial difficulties, had asked his brothers and sisters to help him out. Only Cecil had helped to finance him, hence the relationship between John and Cecil Moores. Sir John, in appreciation, had passed 30 per cent of equity in the company to Cecil Moores and subsequently his descendants.

The relative was the son of one of Sir John's sisters, who was not one of those who supported Sir John in his hour of financial need. There were a number of such people, as it was a very large family. He had some sort of ambition to establish himself as being in the mainstream of family affairs, and had made many allegations, the principal one being that this Managing Director paid higher prices for merchandise when he could easily have bought via other agents from the same supplier, and therefore there must be something in it for him. This was a very doubtful conclusion because price is not the only factor; you would not buy a product unless you were sure of service and support from the supplier.

In effect the allegations were totally groundless and the whole matter had been a waste of management time. With Sir John's blessing, the matter was dismissed after about eighteen months. I subsequently got to know the individual involved quite well. If I had been that well acquainted with him initially, I would have dismissed the implication immediately.

I raise this just by way of illustrating what kind of company it is and I deal in my next chapter at length on the Moores family.

The Littlewoods business in 1983 was in desperate straits with the exception of Pools, which had made a token profit, being a cost plus business. The retail businesses, which are the major part of Littlewoods, were losing substantial money. Debt had risen to £500 million and the bank covenants were exceeded or threatened. Some remedial action had been taken a year or so earlier, and the numbers of staff had been reduced. By and large these had been people in the mainstream of the business, on the productive side, and therefore efficiency had fallen as a consequence of that redundancy programme.

I introduced the normal contemporary management techniques of communication, planning and systems. I set up an extensive review of all parts of the business in an attempt to tackle the problems. I was aware of a lack of morale right through the Company.

The nature of the culture was almost feudal. All the members of the family were addressed by the prefix Mr (Christian name). People were clearly terrified of offending these people as they would be demoted or have to leave the company for what to me were rather minor failings. My initial task was to visit every building, which included all the stores, the Pools offices and the mail order operations in the company, and to meet as many of the 30,000 staff as possible.

This was an invigorating process for me and possibly the staff as the people in the Company were very committed and dedicated, and for their part they were pleased to see somebody new with enthusiasm, experience, and hopefully a sense of leadership.

I set in process a whole variety of management actions. The main thrust of the regeneration was a new five year corporate plan. Indeed the business soon became revitalized and far more confident.

After about a five year period the cash liabilities were paid back and the profit moved towards the £100 million mark, principally from the retail business. There were many tasks to tackle.

Littlewoods paradoxically, because of the heavy traffic through its stores, its very large Pools base and extensive mail order business, probably handled between 20 million and 50 million transactions per week depending on the time of year, and was by any standards a massive company.

I called for an extensive review and examination of the methods of administration. They had been predominantly clerical up to that time and the use of computers had been very largely in conventional stocktaking processes. The business needed to be heavily mechanized, and quickly. Part of this process was already starting in the mail order side in terms of mechanizing the package handling aspects of serving the mail order customers.

In particular the whole process of ordering, supply, delivery throughput to customers, re-stocking, stock control and merchandizing was done, from a computer standpoint, on a primitive or, in computer jargon, 'batch' basis. We set about an extensive programme of re-design of the computer systems.

A substantial investment in computer systems was made to eliminate tons and tons of paper and to bring terminals on to people's desks to give them a real time understanding of whatever it was in the business they were handling. This was no easy task because retailers are unusual in that very few people have other than the basic education. Graduates are almost unknown. People tend to go straight from school into retail and have a natural aversion to new ideas and new techniques. This was exactly the opposite of Plessey where a very high proportion of the staff were graduates and had a natural thirst for change and technological development.

It wasn't unusual on Monday mornings to find in the lifts, trolleys loaded high with great print-outs and it was my determination to eliminate this. Quite apart from the waste of money it struck me that very little of the information was being used and would be better used on an exception basis through a terminal. Having complained bitterly about these print-outs they started to disappear from the Monday morning lift, and I complimented myself on making progress. In reality what had happened was that they were going up by the goods lift at the back of the building so that I did not see them. So nothing had really changed and the staff continued to be unenthusiastic about computer terminal use.

Progressively the terminals rose from six to something in the region of two or three hundred, but again it was clear that they weren't using these terminals and preferred to have the print-out. One day I passed a member of staff who was writing down information from the screen on to a piece of paper. I asked him why he was doing that. He said he was frightened and concerned that he wouldn't be able to find that page again on the computer.

It seemed that not only was the technology necessary to speeding up the business, but also an extensive training programme. This programme extended from the senior management right through the staff and I think that at one stage or another practically every member went through a re-training programme to help them to do their job and in particular to use the new computer automated techniques.

The employees took to it and enjoyed it. The stock turnover levels increased from 6 to about 12 times per year, substantially improving the cash flow. The out of stocks diminished and in the two retail businesses, efficiency in performance improved substantially.

Turning to our financial administration I was also able to recruit a new finance director. He took a look at our banking arrangements and visited our bank on a number of occasions. It was odd to me that we had only one bank and hadn't changed it in the entire life of the company. It was also clear to me that with the enormous number of transactions and the price we were paying per transaction, which was about to be increased, we were paying far too much for our banking service. So we took the extraordinary step, as it seemed to the Company, to go out and tender the whole variety of our banking services which subsequently led to two banks servicing the company and a considerable reduction in banking charges.

Likewise our pension fund, which had been run in-house by Littlewoods directors, had normally performed poorly over a twenty year period. One year, by exception, it out-performed its comparators. This quirk had happened because most of the pension investments were in gilts and that was a very good gilt year, whereas equities are normally the best investment.

We organized a 'pension fund beauty parade' and split the fund, which was by any standards quite a large one, between Schroders and Warburgs, and increased substantially the value of the fund in subsequent years.

Much was done, and could be done in terms of livening up the company.

In 1984, amongst others, we launched into a 'Better Made in Britain' campaign which meant that we would give a price advantage to British companies supplying from Britain. This in effect offset the transport and insurance cost of procuring from abroad. It wasn't a great success because the strange thing about British companies is that they don't want large, long-run orders, nor do they particularly want a process where you want late repeats. This of course is exactly what retailers wanted in the 1980s: high volume, low cost, opportunity to repeat good selling lines.

I often wondered why the manufacturers were not able to respond to this. I think by and large it was attributed to two reasons. Most of the big manufacturers were locked into Marks & Spencer who at that stage would not allow them, except from separate premises, to supply to other retailers.

Secondly the the financial structure of most of these manufacturing companies was restricted by working capital limitations so they seldom had sufficient money to stock up the raw materials for long runs. It seemed to me yet another example where some thought should be given to the financing of the small/medium sized companies, with longer term fixed loans.

The Pools business was an interesting activity. It had been started as the original business of Littlewoods. Contrary to the popular view that it was postal, its principal strength was its very large collector organization which every week took about 85 per cent of the coupons, the balance being by standing forecast. This means you could put your pools in for a period of 50 weeks if you wanted, and the small remaining residue of coupons by post.

There are many interesting stories about the Pools, particularly about the winners, what they did and did not do.

The Pools at this stage was ironically obsessed with the prospect of being nationalized. It seemed to me at the time a totally out-dated point of view. The Conservative Government had been in office for nearly four years. The prospect of them nationalizing it to my mind was zero, but the prospect of competition arising, which was more likely a consequence of the Conservative Government, was very real.

It was quite strange how they refused to accept this possibility, or even this argument. They were convinced that somehow or other the Government would take them over and they would run it. In reality of course as time progressed it became ever more obvious that the Government did intend to introduce competition in the form of the National Lottery.

The National Lottery was gaining credibility. All the old arguments: we were the only country in the world that didn't have a lottery, bearing in mind that the nineteenth century lottery for the British Museum, which was the last one, had been a gigantic fraud. The lottery idea was particularly peddled by the Arts lobby, which was quite influential in Conservative Government circles. They saw this as a wonderful opportunity to raise large sums of money from public sources for the funding of the Arts, against little or no prospect of the Treasury improving its grants to the Arts Council and other institutions.

We spent many hours attempting to convince the Government of the merits of the Pools business. It was difficult to become addicted to Pools as a conscious effort had to be made to place a stake. Substantial sums of money were going from the Pools to the Football Trust for the rebuilding of football grounds and football stadiums. The Pools was a large employer of people because of the heavy paperwork nature of the product. When lotteries are introduced they create endemic gambling habits, particularly in the lower income groups, especially the kind of lottery that was brought into Britain, with its additional scratch card promotion.

This lobbying had some effect, when at quite short notice we agreed, with the Chancellor, to further help fund the Sports and Arts Foundation. While Margaret Thatcher was Prime Minister we seemed reasonably safe from the prospect of a lottery. Indeed she said, quite strongly, in the House of Commons: 'No lottery for Britain.'

Following John Major's appointment, and particularly with Kenneth Baker's enthusiasm, it was becoming clearer and clearer that the prospect of resisting the lottery was going to be difficult. It was claimed to have a wide public appeal, particularly among women who by and large found football pools either uninteresting or too complicated.

A great debate took place with Peter Brook, who became the first Minister for Heritage, doing our very best to diminish the prospect of the severe impact on the Pools of a national lottery. Many promises were made but in reality very little was achieved. The Lottery became a fact, the Pools prospects became diminished and as predicted some years earlier, competition was the danger, not nationalization.

The most profitable and probably, from a business standpoint, the most successful business of Littlewoods was its mail order division, subsequently renamed Home Shopping Division. This business was started after the Pools business had been established in the 1930s and Sir John was looking for a way to use his cash flow to business advantage. He spent some time with the Sears Corporation in America on whom he modelled the future Littlewoods Company. Sears were the largest catalogue company in America.

The mail order business is an embedded credit business. In other words the customer pays for his credit in the price of the goods he purchases. This makes the actual price of the goods substantially higher in the mail order catalogues than in the stores themselves, but the convenient method of payment more than compensates for this higher price.

It works on the basis of agents. An agent may only have, on average, including herself, three customers. Payments were made by the agent and used to be weekly payments, now monthly. The agent is allowed credit on a 1,000 page catalogue of something in the region of 8,000 items, for her and her two customers to buy and pay over twenty or up to sixty weeks, depending on the ticket value of the item sold.

Clearly most clothes were in the 20-week terms, but elaborate hi-fi systems and televisions or even for that matter carpets, could be on the 60-week credit terms. Mail order, as the words imply, meant the items were ordered by mail, delivered by post and payments subsequently made by mail. This arrangement clearly by the early 1980s was out of date, compared with the fast growing high street – new companies, new outlets, and the beginnings of a substantial out of town retail sector.

Major changes were made. A customer could pay by cheque through her bank account, which made payment easier. Secondly, in particular because of postal strikes, a large in-house delivery service of over 2,000 vehicles was created, operating through ten distribution centres round the country, offering a three day delivery service from receipt of order, and if a customer was prepared to pay a premium price, even a 24 hour service.

Welcoming a Russian Tall Ship in Liverpool, 1993.

Enormous changes were made to the computing systems. Previously the customer could ring up an order, an item – shall we say a yellow dress – which could be processed, and then, even on the same day or later, decide to order a red dress instead. The yellow dress ordered couldn't be cancelled so consequently she would receive both the red and the yellow dress, as the system didn't allow an order number to be changed once it had been initiated. The customer resented receiving an item they thought they had cancelled. The so-called handshaking computer system was installed, which allowed the Littlewoods operator, on an interactive conversational mode with the customer, to change the colour of the dress or any aspect of the order, to stop the shipment of the yellow dress and replace it with the red one. The system was designed so that the customer would not know they were speaking to a different person from the one with whom they had actually placed the order.

It was nearly ten years before these interacting handshaking systems were introduced into other industries, for instance banking, the utilities and insurance. They set up what they designated call centres to provide a comparable service.

Furthermore the whole process of the order being placed, instructions to the warehouses, the collection from the warehouse, the wrapping, the distribution to the main sorting house, to the secondary sorting house and into the transport system, was all constantly monitored for the 60 million orders per annum. Therefore the customer service was enormously enhanced in terms of delivering the product that they wanted and which fitted their current requirements regardless of what they had originally asked for.

A very important aspect of the mail order business is to return from the customer's premises as soon as possible, goods that they do not wish to keep. Indeed the proficiency of this was almost as important in the customer's mind as the delivery in the first place because they hated having on their hands something they did not want and might have to pay for. So the returns system, operating in a similar way to the order system, again was interactive with the customer and the goods were removed at an agreed time once the customer decided they did not want them.

There were three million agents and the catalogues themselves consisted of 1,000 pages averaging about £1 million per annum sales for each individual page. The arrangement was broken up into apparel in the first half, and a variety of goods, household, sporting, gardening, fishing etc. in the so-called 'back of the book'. Oddly enough, there were a limited number of people that would take a catalogue with each brand name, so the catalogues were branded with five different names – Burlington, Janet Fraser, J & C Moores, Littlewoods, Peter Craig – to ensure the widest number of agents. The five brand names had an identical 1,000 pages inside.

It is a very efficient form of retail selling. Quite often the agent would order three of a kind, for instance three blouses, with the view to returning two, depending on how they suited her and how the colour looked. But invariably they would only return one, because a relative or friend would take the other one. Consequently a hit rate of two out of three was far more successful than in a high street store itself, where probably twelve dresses were examined before one purchase was made.

The main market was the C2s and Ds and the key to financial success was to balance market share against bad debt. Littlewoods had the second largest market share after GUS, between them accounting for over 60 per cent of the total market. Clearly it was easy to increase sales at the expense of bad debt, and this subtle balancing, I think, was the most relevant factor on the profitability of the business.

It was also a most durable business. Whilst not growing, it had a strong following of customer loyalty, principally mother passing on to daughter the habit of home shopping. And then of course it was supported by a very intensive advertising campaign in the Sunday tabloids to maintain a steady flow of new agents into the business.

At the turn of the 1990s an attempt was made to go to a direct selling catalogue, which was called 'Imagination', the idea being for the younger, more fashionable, women to buy attractive styles and pay directly via credit cards, which they found preferable to the more established credit embedded mail order. Imagination as a business was a fiasco. The catalogues were in great demand and instantly taken up in large numbers but were used more as ladies fashion magazines where the customer contemplated the attractive presentation and bought the goods in the high street. This was an expensive venture for Littlewoods, and was a failure.

The next major business in the Littlewoods organization was the chain store business. There were 108 chain stores in England, Scotland and Wales. The initial two opened before the war but the main thrust was in the 1950s, 60s and 70s to create a chain of stores. Again Sir John was following the Sears of America example of having established the catalogue business and wanting to use the merchandising expertise to create sales in the high street, and also create a portfolio of properties which in post-war Britain was a sound investment constantly increasing in value.

Littlewoods chain stores never really succeeded, although I believe we came close to it around the turn of the 1990s. On visiting all of them in 1984, I found such a rag bag collection and such a gallery of depreciated and dilapidated assets as was hard to imagine. For many years depreciation had not been replaced. The profits – such as they were – had been artificially inflated by lack of depreciation replacement and inflation added to stock depreciation tax allowances which were excessively generous to the retailer.

As always new management was appointed. I was later to learn, as there were in my time probably six Managing Directors of the chain stores, that the most important consideration is, quite simply, the right product at the right price. It does not matter what the appearance of the building is, or any other consideration; if you get the right product at the right price the British shopping public will find it very quickly and you will have substantially increased sales in your business.

All the Managing Directors, except one, followed exactly the same course of action. They would go to consultants for advice, who all produced a chart of which one index was quality and the other was price. They would all show Littlewoods in the wrong quarter in terms of both price and quality. This same chart, from five consultants, I saw five times. It must have cost the company more money than any other piece of paper that they ever had, and yet management constantly looked at it as if it were a brand new discovery. In reality it was the same old turgid advice turned over time and time again.

The management then decided they had to move the price and the quality of its goods up and go for a higher income customer group. This was another fundamental blunder, as Littlewoods' great strength with the C2s and Ds, which is probably the largest market sector, was where it really could make its money. It was quite dangerous to attempt to compete with Marks & Spencer whose customers were prepared to pay higher prices.

So the managers moved what was colloquially known as 'up-market'. The next thing was that they always had to have completely refurbished stores and in particular a new logo and fascia. This is a very expensive business and again quite wrong. The strength of any brand is directly related to its longevity and such brands as Marks & Spencer have hardly changed for many years and is a great strength. Littlewood brand had no x's against it even though it was not seen as exciting. The indelible impression in the consumer's mind is: it is solid, it is sound, it is reliable, it has been there a long time. Indeed almost the last thing you should do in taking over a large chain store group is set about changing the 'image' as they put it or more simply the fascia, which is what indeed was changed.

Chain stores were a constant struggle, a constant disappointment. Indeed Prodip Guha, who was the Group Director of Marketing and who ran the chain store for a few years, had an uncanny sense of striking the balance between cost and quality. Value for money, not exciting but a value-based product. He showed in the early 1990s how a substantial growth could be achieved by sticking to this rather basic policy. Indeed he achieved in 1991 15 per cent growth in the sales when other retailers were making no progress at all.

This policy was not attractive to the management nor, I think, was it attractive to the owners. Everyone was aspiring to be a Liberty's, whereas the real money lay in a Littlewoods' mass market. There is an old saying: 'Work for the masses, live with the classes – work for the classes, live with the masses.' It was Littlewoods' inherent inability to stay in the market that it knew best, namely the mass C2/D markets, with the basic quality products at sensible prices and the inconsistency of holding that approach, that was the principal reason why its chain stores did not prosper.

There were one or two interesting experiments during this period. The smaller stores, called Inside Story, were opened, concentrating principally on inside furnishings, objets d'art and fittings for the home. They didn't make a lot of money, but they didn't lose any either. They were interesting, although there was no heart to expand them through the Group because at the time, in the early 1990s, the cost per square foot of the high street small units increased at an alarming rate, very largely because Next, then run by George Davies, was prepared in the late 1980s to pay any price to get space in town. This had distorted the true value of small high street units.

The peculiar thing about the property market is that all the comparators on rent renewals are based on the highest rent in the town. This highly inflationary practice meant that once rents went up they never came down, and did lead in the middle 1990s to a substantial number of vacant plots due to the early 1990s recession.

Finishing off on Littlewoods Stores: there were some very strong selling lines. For instance, ladies' underwear, hosiery and knitwear were particularly strong. In the food activity, which subsequently abandoned and replaced by an Iceland concession, bacon and cheese were both very good sellers. Lastly the restaurants were the most popular in the high street, as they most certainly did give a good clean efficient service at very competitive prices. They were always full during the principal shopping hours of the day.

The sensible thing for the chain stores was to be merged or sold and, from time to time, there were discussions with other companies but it really meant all or nothing, i.e. all the chain stores were transferred to somebody or you kept them all to ensure sufficient volumes in the purchasing lines to get the right economics. So none of these discussions ever came to anything.

I think the one I most regretted was in the early years of British Home Stores before its merger into Storehouse. BhS and Littlewoods Stores would have been complementary and very efficient had those discussions that took place for some time reached fruition.

The next business was Index catalogue shop, of which over a short period of time about 110 outlets were created. Littlewoods was one of the few companies that understood the catalogue business and managed it profitably. It also had a chain of retail stores. This meant it had the management capacity to run an Argos type catalogue activity. Indeed we approached the owners of Argos (British American Tobacco) with a view to purchasing it, somewhere back in 1985. They had just sold International Stores and were like-minded to sell Argos, but hadn't reached a decision as to what way they would dispose of it, and subsequently floated it on the market. Of course it was a very successful flotation, and has been a very good business. That left us in the position of being a head-on competitor to Argos, bearing in mind we had something in the region of 500 million sales in the mail order, Argos type, products. Nor was it difficult for us to know how to source those products.

At the time of my leaving, Littlewoods Index had yet to prove it was a workable entity. It had the misfortune of being set up in the late 1980s and early 1990s, through a period I have just referred to when the inflation of stores rental shot up at an alarming rate, and by and large they procured space at a much higher cost than the average rental that Argos would be paying. Furthermore, the method of handling stock in catalogue shops is quite different from any other shop. It is on an almost daily stock replacement basis, particularly as you have a high speed low volume stock replenishment programme owing to the fact that stores are quite small and carry a limited number of each line which have to be in stock on a 24 hour basis.

The early days of Littlewoods Index with regard to stock

management replenishment programme was nothing short of chaos, even though we were dealing with only 3000 lines. I recruited an Argos man who had had many years of experience in Tesco stock management. The difficulty was rectified and I would think that given time and patience Index could become a substantial competitor to Argos in a market which it is difficult to enter unless you have high street/ catalogue experiences, which very few other retailers actually have.

The old enemy, GUS, so to speak, watching the development of Index were frustrated in emulating the approach as they had withdrawn from high street retailing. Subsequently, however, they made a successful bid for Argos which will fit well with their Home Shopping.

Another division was set up in the mid 1980s called the International Division. John Martin, then Group Finance director, and I had come to the conclusion that all management action that could be taken in terms of excess manning and all the benefits of new systems were unlikely to show any further improvements in the profit of the company. To this end we studied the gross margins, i.e. the margins available to the company when the goods were received from suppliers, and discovered our gross margins at Littlewoods were the smallest in the retail trade.

We therefore attempted to influence the buying department to improve their commercial buying acumen. This was to no effect as 98 per cent of the buying overseas was done through agents and nobody wanted to dislodge those arrangements. I would refer back to pre 1983 when a far higher percentage was bought direct from manufacturers abroad, but the entire technology and quality control department had been fired.

Littlewoods had no choice but to rely upon agents to inspect the sources for their quality and standards. The agents were told the selling price and they asked for a 30 per cent gross margin and Littlewoods got an equal 30 per cent margin. What the agents themselves received, as they had full control over the manufacturing sources, could have been anything between 30 and 50 per cent.

We visited the Far East and discovered it was generally nearer 50 per cent. In all fairness of course, the agent had his own staff to the extent that he was monitoring and controlling the sourcing of our products. This was not being done very well as a proportion of our product received in the UK was of low quality.

To make a start in overcoming this problem we decided to acquire a small agent in Hong Kong named Harris who had owned his operation and sold goods to Littlewoods. Harris stayed as a consultant and had a previously quite unique arrangement in that he was simply paid a salary to pass the goods to us at the price at which he bought them.

By the turn of the decade, following discussions with the Chinese Embassy, we attempted to increase our sourcing from China following meetings with the Northern Industry Company of China, the largest manufacturing company, and the early 1990s we signed an agreement which was really a protocol to attempt to get Norenco, as it was called, to produce goods not just for Littlewoods, but for us to sell in the European countries to other retailers. Norenco had originally been a military products company and had been converted by the Chinese Government to the manufacture of domestic products. We for our part were to help them specifically in the area of kitchen appliances and customize them for European standards and Littlewoods would handle sales to Continental Europe.

China was chosen because the agents had locked us out of the principal market sources of Hong Kong and we knew it was necessary to go to other countries. Eventually a further agreement was signed with a company called Lorad, who helped or managed Littlewoods sourcing arrangements into other countries such as Thailand, the Philippines, Bangladesh and Indonesia, areas in which the agents did not have at that point a stranglehold on the manufacturing sources. There were various points of view as to whether this activity was a success. What clearly was, was the sales growth coming directly from these new initiatives which towards the middle of the 1990s was somewhere in excess of £50 million, a remarkable performance from a very small beginning.

Other major corporate initiatives were of value, and I will mention just a few.

Home Shopping Division had built up its own very large transport fleet. This transport fleet was still costing, on a cost per parcel, too high a price to this division.

We engaged consultants, I believe they were Kearneys, who were instructed to find a purchaser for our 2,000 strong home delivery service in our Home Shopping Division, and enter into a five year binding contract with a 15 per cent reduction in cost of the parcels delivered.

Kearneys turned up with two real prospective purchasers. One was the Post Office, whose labour relations gave us some concern; and the other was the American Company, Federal Express, who were keen to establish a large operating base in the United Kingdom on which to build a larger parcels business.

After discussions we visited Federal Express in Memphis, Tennessee, the home of Elvis, and were absolutely overwhelmed at the efficiency and magnitude of the US parcels handling activity. They had a larger plane fleet, of 747 and DC10 and various types of aircraft, than British Airways. These arrived and departed every night from Memphis and parcels were transferred after sorting to different planes.

They had grown, under the chairmanship of Fred Smith, from virtually nothing to become the world's major operator in parcel handling and delivery. We were guests at their sales conference. The mood and the atmosphere of enthusiasm of all their staff was infectious and left me in no doubt that here we had a company whose management could really transform our home shopping delivery service.

The lawyers of both parties sat for two weeks in conclave to finalize the most exhaustive agreements, before we sold to Federal Express the assets of our Home Delivery Service at fair value. They entered into agreement to provide a delivery of the parcels at a 15 per cent lower price than we could do ourselves. This to us was an excellent arrangement but Federal Express failed to build the business in the UK. Whether they couldn't find the right management, or whether it was really the practice of most UK companies preferring to have their own delivery service that frustrated them, I do not know.

But two years later we were offered the same business back by Federal Express for compensation equalling the three years outstanding delivery commitments and assuring the 15 per cent discount was carried through to the end of the five year period. This to me was an excellent arrangement because, during the two year period of tenure in which they managed the home delivery service, they had applied their modern computer based efficient management techniques and substantially enhanced the quality of operation for us. In other words, we lent them the business at a reduced cost for two years and got it back in much better shape and with a large bounty, over £40 million, to go with it. It was an excellent corporate transaction, of great value to Littlewoods.

Early in the 1990s the deputy chairman of Leningrad, soon to be called St. Petersburg, visited me in Liverpool to create an interest in opening retail stores in St. Petersburg itself. Somebody was sent to examine this possibility and returned with favourable comment. Shortly afterwards Mr Subcick, the Mayor of St. Petersburg, visited the north west of England, which gave me the chance to spend a day with him and show his party the Littlewoods Stores. Mrs Subcick in particular was absolutely ecstatic and, probably having looked at other stores in the UK, observed that Littlewoods Stores had exactly the right sort of merchandise and realistic pricing that would suit the ladies of St. Petersburg.

We shook hands and subsequently opened a number of stores, in fact six, in St. Petersburg. They didn't make any money, but again they didn't lose any money, and they really were the foundation of a future Russian business.

The main difficulties in Russia were the high level of inflation and the fact that the currency could not be repatriated, therefore imports to Russia were in hard currency whereas all dealings were in local currency. It was a constant drain on Treasury management to keep a balance in spite of the fact that some of the goods were actually made in Russia itself.

Another initiative was that we had had some discussions with

UNEDO both in the UK and in Vienna where they are based. UNEDO (United Nations Economic Development Organization) were particularly keen on certain Far East and African countries providing financial support for the development of manufacturing operations to improve the local economy in those countries. This fitted in with our desire for new sources of procurement directly from manufacturers as opposed to agents, but regrettably whilst these discussions seemed quite hopeful at one stage, we lacked sufficient management resources to make them happen in the countries identified.

In addition we became a British member of RIMPRO, which is the European trade association, and particularly with the French and the Germans much discussion took place with regard to exchanging information on product sources. The Germans import a lot of products from Eastern Europe from where we import very little. We for our part procured most of our products from the Far East. These discussions, particularly with the French, looked quite hopeful early on.

It can be seen from all this that Littlewoods had changed dramatically from being an insular, failing company in the early 1980s to being a recognized growing, successful business with much wider contacts and influence in the early 1990s.

It was against this background that I thought that my ten years as Chief Executive had been more than sufficient and I felt the need for a change. It had not been a happy company to work for because of the feudal nature of the owners, the Moores Family, which I describe in more detail in the next chapter.

My ten years as Chief Executive of Littlewoods can, I believe, be regarded as both a personal success and a company success. As I've outlined earlier, the fortunes of the company multiplied during my service, whilst as Chief Executive it had its moments. It was good to see the business results at the end of my period of tenure. I felt I should retire as Chief Executive in April 1993, but it was suggested by the Littlewoods Board that I should stay on as non-Executive Vice Chairman. This idea appealed to me for sentimental reasons. You don't easily walk away from something that you've given ten years of your life to, where you've made many friends, with whom you have developed an attachment, having worked with them over a long period of time.

For me to be appointed non-Executive Vice Chairman of Littlewoods required the majority consent of the shareholders. There was a strong caucus of these that wanted me to take this position in the interest of continuity. There was equally a group that felt that it was better for all concerned if I completely severed my relationships with the company. In the event the majority was for me to take the position. It was a secret ballot so I do not know the exact results, but I suspect it was a thin majority at the time. With hindsight, and as Sir John Moores always used to say, 'it's a great shame we haven't got foresight as good as our hindsight,' it probably would have been better for me and all concerned if the majority had been against the appointment.

At the time my successor was Barry Dale, who had been the Group Finance Director. He was appointed, coincidentally, at almost the same time Sir John Moores died. This resurrected the struggle inside the company, which was to lead to severe friction over the next two or so years. The second generation of family members on the Board wanted to re-assert the influence of the family on the business, wishing to control the management to a point which would have diminished its effectiveness. Barry, being the new Chief Executive, wanted to establish his position and authority and set about it with a series of bold, good decisions and with enthusiasm to do just that. It was not a comfortable existence. In effect as non-Executive Vice Chairman of the company, the shareholder directors viewed me as a supporter of the management: having come from there they still saw me as part of it and a supporter of the Executive Directors. The Executive Directors themselves saw me as a fifth columnist to the family directors and consequently neither the family directors nor the Executive Directors spoke to me. I lived in an existence of not communicating with anybody or really having any idea of what was going on inside the business, or of the prospective decisions that might emerge from

behind the scenes. I chose to ignore this vacuum and would appear at
the monthly Board meetings on a regular basis, make whatever
contribution I could make and let them get on with it. In May 1995 I
resigned.

CHAPTER 7

The Moores Family

LET ME GO THROUGH my relationships as I understood them with the Moores family, starting with Sir John Moores.

Sir John was a remarkable man if at times his actions caused embarrassment. He was eighty-seven years old when I joined The Littlewoods Organization. Over the years that followed his faculties were nothing short of impressive. I speak quite quietly and also carry an accent. This means that from time to time some people ask me to repeat myself. In the years with Sir John there was never an occasion that he didn't understand first time exactly what I was talking about and his speech was so lucid and clear that there was never any lack of comprehension.

If I had any hope of running The Littlewoods Organization effectively, I had to have his hundred per cent support. It was a high risk policy but I could see no other.

There were various encounters and discussions at the beginning, but after a reasonably short period he, without qualification, gave me his entire wholehearted support. He did this by pronouncing to the staff in particular, and the managers, that I was the boss and that everybody, including himself, had to do what I told them to do.

He had what I think was a really unwarranted view of me as a manager, based on his statement that Sawyer and I were the two people in his entire life who saved him being out of work and on the street. Sawyer had been the Managing Director with him during the forties and the fifties, when Littlewoods made a major contribution to the war effort which he felt was never properly recognized.

My relationship with him was always formal. I called him Sir John and he called me Mr Pitcher and I didn't attempt to trespass into his

private feelings. That would have killed the relationship and recipro-
cally I too wished to retain my independence, if I was to be an effective
Chief Executive of the business.

Sir John didn't really have much of a sense of humour and this was
illustrated one day when an incident took place in the company lift. He
would come into the office two or three times a week, arriving promptly
at 9.30 a.m, having an early lunch and leaving thereafter. On one of these
occasions he burst into my office, which was a very unusual thing for
him to do, proclaiming loudly that there was a lunatic in the building. I
didn't think this would be too unusual. With three thousand people
working in a building there are bound to be one or two odd people. The
cause of Sir John's consternation, it emerged, was a man who seemed to
be in the lift most mornings at 9.30 when he was coming in. On this particular morning Sir John had apparently challenged the chap by saying,
'Late again,' to which the employee had replied, 'Yes, so am I, Sir John.'

The nature of my relationship with Sir John was really threefold.
The first part was management itself. He had formed quite an incorrect
impression of my ability in this field, very largely because he had never
had any managers with contemporary experience, the previous ones
having been recruited internally. My work in planning, communications, motivation and systems intrigued him enormously. He was quite
capable of picking up substantial reports and recommendations,
analysing them in depth and enjoying a long debate with a unique
insight which was helpful and interesting.

The second part of our relationship came about because I actually
joined Littlewoods quite simply for personal motives, to try to save my
second marriage, spend more time at home and live a more settled
domestic existence.

In reality that plan failed as did the marriage. So I really had time on
my hands apart from working full time, and because nobody else
would, I accompanied him to various football matches, in both
Liverpool and other cities. We both enjoyed our football and discussed
it at quite some length, and from time to time we shared watching
international games on television.

The third element of the relationship, which at times was distasteful to me, was his preoccupation with discussing his family with me. Rightly or wrongly, and the situation may have been of his own making, he was very bitter and felt very let down by his family. He had four children.

His eldest son, John, who had fallen out with his father after the failure of a major acquisition in Germany – some say it wasn't John's fault – he described him as a nice boy, but a soft touch and gullible. John was excessively nervous in his father's company.

His other son, Peter, whom he had fired as the previous Executive Chairman, shortly before my appointment, he described as a man who had no sense of other people's feelings and reactions and was sometimes offensive in the way in which he conducted himself. He was very angry over Peter's homosexual inclinations which Peter had tried to keep from his father. His father, being what he was, tried to find out where he was living and who he was living with. He got angry and distraught about the situation. His eldest daughter was Lady Grantchester, married to Kenneth, a distinguised QC. He was Recorder of the Crown Court and Chairman of Value Added Tax tribunals. He constantly harped on about Betty's peculiar comments and talked of the mistake he had made bringing her onto Littlewoods' main board.

He hardly commented on Janatha, the youngest daughter, as she played no role in the business.

Maybe it was his own mistake, but he had passed most of his shareholding down through the family to limit inheritance tax liabilities. This meant that a large number of the family including the third generation had a substantial shareholding, which had limited transferability and only token yield. Sir John did not want this arrangement changed. He openly and frequently declared resentment about the fact that these people had done nothing for the company and seemed to think, as he put it, that they owned it, which of course they did, but Sir John did not wish to recognize that.

My relationship with Sir John went on until about 1992. His faculties then started to fail quite dramatically.

John Moores, Sir John's elder son, is indeed a very likeable person, but can switch his affections quite suddenly and frequently. John supported my method of running the company and for my part I tried to promote his own particular interests of non discrimination against women and ethnic minorities and we embarked upon some very interesting programmes. My motivation was that the more skills available to compete in management and elsewhere, the better it was for the company. His motivation was highly moral and very dedicated. John, in a sense, particularly after his father lost his faculties, was really a very isolated man in The Littlewoods Organization and sometimes this caused him difficulties.

His brother Peter, who in theory had left The Littlewoods Organization but had retained substantial interests through trusts and share ownership could, if he wanted, be ingratiating on a particular point but could also be offensive, either intentionally or by accident,

My relationship with Betty, Lady Grantchester, was never an easy one. My council house background, in spite of my extensive international management experience over twenty years, and my interest in working class issues, contrasted with her very privileged upbringing. Betty kept things very close to herself. She never revealed her thoughts or opinions and would, in conjunction with Peter, attempt to manipulate activities inside the company or associated with it.

I really fell out with Betty in the middle of 1993. I was by then Deputy Chairman of Everton Football Club and Chairman of its Finance Committee and had been promoting recapitalization of the Club as performance and fortunes were failing badly in the Premier League. This I had done in conjunction with Betty who had the Power of Attorney acting for her father who was incapable at this stage to enter into any coherent debate. We seemed to be getting nowhere and I had pursued, with outside bankers, the prospect of finding a Godfather to bring substantial financial direction to the Club.

Sir John owned 40 per cent of the equity and no new equity had been issued for 120 years. The attempt to go outside led to Betty abstaining in the vote for my re-election at one of the AGMs. I naturally took exception to this; we had a major disagreement and never really spoke to each other from that point.

The real problem, however, started at the end of 1994. We had found two prospective Godfathers, one of whom was very real, Peter Johnson then having wealth of between £100 and £200 million. He was hi-jacked by Betty's advisers and told to deal with the shareholders and not with the Board. This was a very unsatisfactory arrangement, but on the other hand if it led to a fresh injection of cash that would have been acceptable.

In the meantime, Betty entered into a secret agreement with a director of the Everton Board to bring in her son, and other outside advisers, putting in a small amount of recapitalization. The Board in turn, one by one, were induced or encouraged to take her position and support her offer. We were never advised properly or formally of the secret agreement, save by the Director of the Club who was a party to it.

I went straight back to Johnson and discovered he was in the end prepared to offer £4,000 per share and put £10 million into the Club to get a controlling interest. A vicious battle then ensued inside the Board between the Pro-Granchesters and myself, acting in what I believed to be the only proper interest of the other shareholders and insisting they obtain the highest possible price for the shares. In the end the others finally gave way. Johnson came in and took over the Club. It was of course a final blow to any possible hopes of me enjoying a relationship with Betty Grantchester.

That I think is a 'birds eye' view of my relationships with the family and firm as they come to mind at this later time.

It should always be borne in mind, however, that the Moores were a very large family, with very diverse and different outlooks. One tends to concentrate on Sir John and members of the second generation. Certainly some of the members of the third generation are showing a totally different interest in the business and are active, acting much more like shareholders who want the best returns, secure investment and responsible, soundly-based management.

The family decided on the manner in which the company would be run as they were the total owners and were indeed, by any description, very good employers. They insisted on the staff receiving the best consideration *vis-à-vis* equality, pensions, concern for illness and all those paternalistic considerations that only really come in a privately owned company. The pension scheme was as good as any. It was also at an early stage open to part time staff, of which there were quite a few, as the staff was substantially female. There were a whole variety of social events, such as the Arts and Crafts Exhibition, the annual prize-giving for part time education which was much encouraged and rewarded by the company. There were days out for invalid children during the summer from the homes in which the disadvantaged children were residing.

The family shared a dislike of my awful task of having to substantially reduce the employees in the company. They had always seen the employees as an integral part of the business, like any modern well informed employer, and cared very much for their welfare. They had limited redundancies in the past and we followed the pattern, which we substantially achieved, of only having voluntary redundancies. This meant the terms of severance were far better than any other commercial company would have given its staff. Indeed they were keen to do just that.

The Moores Family Charitable Trust, as it was specifically called, made many donations both large and small, which were considered by the family on an annual basis, directing a significant part of the profits to charitable purposes. Young John, Sir John's son, spent a lot of time and probably all his money in Liverpool, particularly helping the underprivileged and the disadvantaged. He was very much supported by his wife Jane, who devoted much of her life to that, as well as considerable time, even at personal risk, helping the black women of South Africa during the difficult times before the end of Apartheid. Peter, the other brother, gave substantial sums to the Arts and Education and to other activities not necessarily of direct interest. He did much to distribute his wealth to the benefit of people who had not got such good opportunities.

In short, like all families, there were good and bad. Some I got on with, some I didn't. One of the good things about running a large privately owned company is that you do not have any problems with decisions. You go straight to the shareholders and get answers and, by and large, I got the support I needed. In terms of the family's attitude to the executives, they paid well; there is no doubt about that. Of all my requests in terms of remuneration for other executives, hardly any were discussed in a questioning way; most were supported without hesitation, having had proper explanations. They didn't like executives who didn't perform. They didn't want them to receive remuneration they weren't entitled to, and they didn't particularly want to see them in the company. They had a very equitable outlook for a shareholder and easily translated when you're working for a company held by the private sector.

I have tried to be balanced in my comments on the Moores family, taking into account they do not like criticism or even comment regarding the Littlewoods Company and themselves.

Sir John's health declined in 1992 and he died in September 1993. During this period his faculties waned, he could not communicate and was permanently confined to bed. I continued to call in but less frequently than I had. It was hard to say if I was any help.

Then one Sunday morning after months of no contact he suddenly spoke. He did not move but spoke in a partly incoherent but some-times clear way and then silence. I waited a while and then decided to leave. As I was leaving he made a statement that was to be his last to me. He was sharing his experience with me in the way he had done many times but this time he was passing on a message which I retain and will not reveal.

As I said, Sir John died in September 1993, never getting full recognition because he disliked media promotion and false social patronage. Being one of the outstanding industrial figures of his era, he was the architect and creator of Littlewoods, the largest British private company by customer numbers and trading activity, and on his death the most profitable private company.

He built it from two to over 30,000 people in seventy years of endeavour. After his death the company was sold by the family in over seven years, the final transaction being in October 2002 with the sale of the stores, Index and Home Shopping.

Seventy years of endeavour sold by his family in seven years: was this disloyalty and financial opportunism? A natural question. But it could have been a shrewd move to let somebody better able than the family own and carry on the difficult management task.

CHAPTER 8

United Utilities

I JOINED THE BOARD of North West Water in 1990 and subsequently became its Deputy Chairman. I assisted as best a non-Executive could in what was the heart of a great change programme initiated by the then Chief Executive, Mr Bob Thian.

That programme was a £300 million quality and efficiency project centring around a complex of modern buildings and a major information technology system. It was innovative and interesting and it was a pleasure to play a part in it.

The facilities themselves consisted of some, although not all, of the following. First was a new fully automated laboratory capable of handling 3 million samples per year. The whole lot handled previously only partially and inadequately in 28 small laboratories in different parts of the region. The complexity of the task that could be undertaken in the new laboratory and the speed of response made it probably the most advanced water and sewage analysis laboratory in the world.

The second was a customer services premises not unlike the handshaking developments that we had undertaken at Home Shopping in Littlewoods. The customer could ring up for all manner of queries from bills to burst pipes to service engineer arrangements. By dealing with one person on the telephone customers could get the feeling of friendly service on a personal basis.

Third was a control centre for the whole of the water and sewage network for the North West, which could be monitored for output and quality by one central location in Warrington. This task, particularly the information technology aspect, was a five year programme of enormous magnitude involving many consultants and others, which really took until 1997 to complete. It was the most significant quantum jump in any company in terms of technological transformation, and improvement of efficiency and quality.

The water industry in which I was to find myself became not only a political football but also a media plaything. Much of the work of the chairman, which I became on 31 March 1993, was more akin to the work of a political lobbyist or even of a politician, with all the ramifications arising from being in the political arena.

There was much said about the privatization of water, but the plain fact of the matter was that it was an absolute necessity by 1989. The infrastructure was crumbling due to lack of maintenance and replacement. Indeed the renewal programme was one of a 150 year term and most of it was 100 years old. It was a naive hope that something in the region of 200 years old would continue to be serviceable and useable. The 150 year programme was based on the Treasury's inclination to spend, rather than on the realities of the condition of the infrastructure itself. Furthermore, much of the sewage went out to sea or to rivers. The new World Health/EEC standards for water of 50 tests was being forced upon the British, to bring reasonable standards for water and proper handling of sewage.

North West Water itself was faced with a bill of £11 billion if it were to tackle its obligations properly, and at privatization a real cost increase of 5 per cent was fixed on the price to attempt to fund the capital. The size of the task and a cash flow income from an increased pricing was an enormous management challenge to which, in my belief, North West Water management magnificently responded.

They first of all acquired a number of water process manufacturing companies, for instance Wallace and Tiernan, who were the world's earliest firm in water treatment (in fact they started the whole process way back in the 1930s). This gave North West Water special experience in water purification processes.

They also acquired Envirex, which had 25 per cent of the US market in sewage management. Again those techniques were applicable to the North West Water sewage system designs. General Filter was another acquisition, and gave a much higher understanding of the current technology levels of sewage and water filtration.

Wallace & Tiernan and Envirex were world wide companies operating in Germany, England, the USA, Mexico and Australia, amongst other countries.

The second task that North West Water undertook was an analysis of the capital spend, to see how in the design process it could cut the costs further.

Lastly there were the so-called quadripartite discussions with the Government, the Economic Regulator who set the prices and assured the outputs, the National Rivers Authority, and the Environmental Regulator who ensured that the effluent standards to the rivers were satisfactory. They were further able to derogate certain capital programmes until the next century. Thereby with a combination of new know-how, increased design efficiency and Government consultation, the level building came down nearer to a £7 billion capital investment programme.

This was still probably the largest capital investment programme ever undertaken over a period of that duration by any British Company. The one exception was the Channel Tunnel, which was an Anglo-French company.

Prices for water had been kept artificially depressed and were much lower than in comparative countries. Politicians made great play of the fact that water prices went up, whilst ignoring the massive investment programme. They also talked a lot about the increased level of remuneration of the directors, whilst disregarding the fact that practically all the management were new, with contemporary advanced management techniques and experience, being paid generally below their market value. Politicians emphasized the increase in value of Executives' Share Options since privatization.

There was nothing particularly new in that flotation situation, but from a previous public sector company it somehow or other was seen to be improper. The people who benefited, the original management, had left the industry but the new management who joined after privatisation were tagged with the same suggestion of unfair and unreasonable share option benefits, which they didn't receive.

Much was said of exaggerated salaries. These were either completely inaccurate facts or simply dishonest statements for political gain: more about winning General Elections. No mention was made of the major improvements in the water industry quality and ultimately in reduced costs, none of which would have been possible, or even contemplated, under a Treasury managed water industry, as it had been prior to 1989.

Conscious of the need for on-going cash flow on a regulated business – as far as I could see water would always be a monopoly – we endeavoured to acquire BOOT contracts, which stands for Build Own and Operate sewage or water treatment plants, for up to thirty years in overseas countries. In this we were successful; we secured, quite early in 1993, major contracts in Melbourne and Sydney; and subsequently contracts in Bangkok, the Philippines and Macau, and additionally in Mexico City. With the acquisition of a company called US Water came a variety of small contracts which I believe will lead to larger ones in major US cities. These long term contracts would lead to the flow of inward capital to the UK, and the creation of work in the UK to support the jobs and management activities in the overseas countries.

The biggest contract of all was that for the national sewage operations in Malaysia, which we did in conjunction with a consortium. Two of the partners were the Police and Army Pension Funds. This involved the complete service to the 17 million population of Malaysia and was, and probably will be for a long time, the largest ever contract acquired outside Europe by a European Water Company.

This overseas contract set the scene for a large unregulated business, although it would take time to grow owing to the connection rates and the build up of the revenue from the different countries.

We felt that we wanted to change the nature of the company and indeed we did, by the acquisition of NORWEB. This utility in the North West served 80 per cent of North West Water's customers. At the same time it was a privatized utility, still apparently a monopoly. That was not actually true as half of NORWEB's business is over 100 kilowatts in size, and is totally competitive on a national basis from other so-called RECs (Regional Electricity Companies), and of course NORWEB itself could compete outside its own area.

In 1998 the domestic market became competitive. From then on the entire NORWEB business was wholly competitive. This meant that by the year 2000 the majority of our business would be non regulated. Taking the NORWEB acquisition and the overseas business, as little as 35 per cent would be regulated after that period.

If one company provides for all utility services, water, electricity, gas and telephone, it is much more efficient. In addition to water and electricity, NORWEB had progressed into the provision of gas and both North West Water and NORWEB had presence in telecommunications. As only one head office and one administrative infrastructure are needed, the merger should lead to much lower overhead costs.

That was the basic rationale for the merger, but the vehicle for its achievement was the major information technology programme started back in 1991. We formed a company called Vertex which was able to provide all the administrative and operational management services from billing to the supervision of road works and the control of the transport fleets, in the most modern organized manner. The vehicle or

Study Group, Future of Work, Trade Union friends.

the engine of change to get these efficiencies and improve customer services was the Vertex company.

Interestingly enough a utility company in Cedar Falls, Iowa, USA with a population of 36,700 has set a trend in motion in the States for water, electricity, gas and telecommunication companies to become multi-utilities. It is said that many smaller utility companies are following their example there because of the benefits and virtues of such an arrangement. It probably confirms that the time has come for the multi-utility, particularly in the Western countries.

The multi-utility concept was very attractive from the customer's standpoint, and from that of a shareholder provided the company could be made to operate as a genuine multi-utility and not simply a group of separate services. A very interesting discussion took place on this with the responsible executive of the World Bank when we jointly gave a presentation to an international audience.

The real business advantage of a multi-utility comes from the cash flow. The investment with the fastest return is telecommunications

Duke of Edinburgh's visit to United Utilities Control Centre, 1996.

because the revenue per capital spend is far higher than for gas and electricity, and substantially higher than water, which has the lowest revenue per capital spend of the four. Consequently, if you put the four utilities together, you can use the cash flow generated by telecommunications and to some extent the lesser, but important, cash flow generated by gas and electricity to fund the ever increasing burden of capital spend needed on water and in particular on sewage. The World Bank considered taking this forward as an idea when countries applied for aid, as they invariably applied for aid for telecommunications and put water quite low on their list of priorities. This meant people had telephones without water and definitely without proper sewage and sanitation. The multi-utility funding arrangement, and the better management of a multi-utility, would mean a progressive increase in the facilities and standards available to citizens in the developing countries. It may seem odd that someone would prefer having a telephone to running water, but many people in countries in South East Asia get themselves a television well before they have any running water supply.

By this stage we actually had in place a new Chief Executive who played a major role in the acquisition of the NORWEB electric company. He was Brian Staples, who had previously been the Managing Director of Tarmac Construction, a major part of the Tarmac Group. With the exception of one non-Executive Director, the Board were all enthusiastic for Brian to take up the position. Brian paid a major part in the acquisition of the NORWEB company and the subsequent rationalization of the Group. We decided to concentrate on the core business of a multi-utility fully integrated in the North West, with our overseas projects.

We sold the generating companies which belonged to NORWEB, taking the view that distribution and generation should probably be separated in the interest of effective competition. We sold the process equipment manufacturing companies in North America and Australia and small plants in Europe for £125 million, which was £50 million more than we had anticipated. Matters were going well. The ideal of achieving a genuinely integrated multi-utility company to achieve customer service, cash flow, profitability and dividends looked very promising.

It is at times like this, when things are going well and the future looks exciting, that you tend to miss the black clouds which are forming on the horizon. There were two, one external and one internal. Externally the Labour Party in Opposition was making great play of the 'Fat Cat' issue. The principal starting point was the substantial salary increase for Cedric Brown when he was appointed to the position of Chief Executive of British Gas. Interestingly enough, his Chairman was paid more than him for a part time position, but because he was American that was considered different and not politically exciting.

Cedric had reached the top of the organization after starting as a trainee, a great achievement indeed. Although I never met him I spoke to him on the phone on a number of occasions and formed the view that he was a capable and pleasant person. There may have been a mistake in that sudden escalation of Cedric's salary, but he had in fact worked there all his life, and it was a very commendable thing that he should have progressed in the way that he did. One might expect his critics to admire that as an opportunity of equality for all people in companies to aspire to the top.

The Labour Party were looking out for someone in the water industry to target, as they felt the public had more antipathy towards water than other nationalized industries. Water is, in a sense, a hidden activity and always appears to come for a relatively low price. They decided I was probably the best person to designate a 'Fat Cat'. They, and the Press that followed them, chose to ignore my many years of wide international business experience, and the fact that I didn't join the industry for money. I was paid substantially less at North West Water than I was at Littlewoods. This was quite a vicious and nasty campaign, misleading the public for political gain. People asked me how I felt about it, and I had several levels of thought. A great deal of what was said in the press was inaccurate and exaggerated. In particular articles written by two female journalists and the Business Editor of one of the broadsheets, who seemed to want to deny his origins from Birkenhead and pretend he'd always been in London society, were bordering on the malicious.

This led to a Select Committee on Employment holding special sessions on executive remuneration. Its purpose was to create publicity and profiles and to give the Labour Party scope to attack the Government for allegedly mishandling the privatization of the utilities and, specifically in my case, water. They were great circuses of media activity and it fell to me to be the third person to speak – or to be interrogated is probably the best description – by the Members of Parliament on that Select Committee. My own personal feelings about that were clearly of resentment. I didn't believe it was right for me as a non political member of the public to be treated by a Select Committee of the House of Commons, as if I was on trial to justify and explain why business functions in the way it does. By and large, in the end, taking into account reactions from other people, I probably did as well as could be done, and the general view was that I gave an effective political response to a political question, thus limiting the scope of the

Being told off by Mrs Thatcher during one of her visits to the north.

politicians to build the class division between management and the staff of a company. After a period of time it died a natural death, although from time to time whenever the subject of 'Fat Cats' comes up in whatever context I tend to figure in the debate.

I think it was the behaviour of industrialists that gave me and many others greater concern. This led to the Greenbury Committee to look at the remuneration of executives. It was often suggested that the Prime Minister asked Greenbury to do this, but I doubt it, because when I ask people to confirm it, they are solidly of the view that no request had ever been made. It was certainly the desire of industrial worthies, generally retired executives, who somehow feel they still represent British industry and can speak for it. They don't accept the fact that many things have moved on since they were effective executives in the industrial scene. The Greenbury enquiry ensured, almost for ever, that executives will always be in for criticism in terms of the rewards they get for their efforts. The scarcity of executives and the specific talents they require will always be disregarded because the Greenbury enquiry in reality appeared to the public to be industry itself agreeing that executive pay was a matter that had gone past the point of reasonableness. The Group itself tried to pass this off as simply a utility problem. In fact it soon became clear, when the press started to produce lots of facts, that the utilities, in many respects, were the least offenders in the escalation of managerial incomes.

I personally took the view that we live in a democratic society, that politicians say what they want because they need the votes, and that the press write the articles because they want to sell papers. You can hardly criticise people for doing their job whatever you may think of what they do or say in the execution of their work. But the situation did get out of hand. Ian McCartney, who subsequently became Minister for Industry, took it upon himself to parade outside the Annual General Meetings with people dressed in cat outfits and carrying deprecating placards. There's no doubt this was entertaining stuff for the television and other media, but it also had another effect that was somewhat disquieting. In the middle of the night in June 1997, fortunately whilst the family was away, our home in Cheshire was fire-bombed by extremists who confirmed that the reason for this action was the 'Fat Cat' issue and who intended to repeat the exercise elsewhere. At the time the damage was played down, but it's not at all a pleasant experience to have your possessions and house attacked in this way in a civilized democratic country. It illustrates to me how easy it is for political extremism, such as that exhibited by McCartney, to reach the point where there is danger to life and limb, not simply to me but to other people. It is interesting that the whole of the 'Fat Cat' issue smacked of Macarthy-ism in the old American form.

The other black cloud was an internal one. Brian Staples, on joining North West Water, had introduced us to his charming third wife Sonia, who was part of his entry in *Who's Who*. It subsequently turned out however that Sonia was not his wife, as he was still married to his second one. This emerged during a very unpleasant episode in the middle of 1996 when it transpired that my recently appointed secretary had, for some time been having an affair with Brian Staples. He had strongly recommended her appointment even though there was a preferred applicant and I was also somewhat encouraged by the then Group Personnel Director who was acting under his instructions. This matter came to light when Brian and my secretary went to Bangkok on a trip when she was supposed to be on holiday in Devon, and of course he was on a business trip. My secretary was also married at the time and it struck me as odd that they both arrived back late, as I had that very morning attempted to contact Brian and spoken to Sonia and to my secretary's husband. This coincidence very quickly led me to confide in two of the non-Executive Board members and brought to light the discovery of this affair. This caused a great deal of unpleasantness and the whole matter was discussed with non-Executives as to what course of action should be taken. Some felt that it was an act of deceit by the Chief Executive to encourage the appointment of his mistress into my office and another group, represented by Sir Peter Middleton, felt that it wasn't really of any importance. Sir Peter Middleton, who had joined the Board some time earlier, held the view that this sort of thing was happening all the time and if every time there was an affair management took some disciplinary action there would be constant disruption to the business. The affair wasn't the point at issue; it was the deception which was the concern, but after a personal discussion with Brian the matter was left in abeyance, the secretary left and obviously the relationship between him and me from that point onwards was never the same.

Becky Sandford then became my Personal Assistant. She was the applicant who had been my preferred choice when I appointed her predecessor. Another earlier secretary was Linda Varnes. I never ceased to be amazed by their ability, competence and reliability and have often wondered if there are obstacles in the way of promotion that stop their abilities from being taken fully into account. I cannot understand why they stayed at this level, as both these ladies could, if given the chance, have played a very effective role in senior management positions. For Becky personally there was some slightly amusing spin-off from the Brian Staples affair. When she told people she used to be my PA, some smiled and said, 'Oh – were you the other woman?' Her natural sense of humour handled this very well.

I return to Sir Peter Middleton, who was a senior civil servant of considerable reputation and on retirement became Deputy Chairman of Barclays Bank; some years later almost by accident he became its Chairman. Before I invited Peter, with the agreement of my colleagues, to join the Board a close confidant of mine made the point that he would never have either civil servants or bankers on his Board as he had found them, by experience, to be less than helpful in terms of constructive advice and support. With Peter of course we had the two and I ignored my confidant's advice.

In a business with millions of customers overall, North West Water/United Utilities had seven million. Littlewoods had a weekly customer base of twenty million rising to over forty million at the end of the year. You have to get to know the psychic image of the customer, what he or she feels is important to them, and to be able to give them the reassurance that the company is concerned about them, and that, in particular, they have access to the management. This is done by the implementation of extensive and easy access customer telephone and letter enquiry systems, a programme of in-depth customer contact, frequently sending out information to them, and continuous and frequent personal contact at all levels of management directly in the field with the customers. United Utilities/North West Water staff and I spent a lot of our time doing just this, to form, based on substantial facts, a comprehensive view of what the customer needed.

At the many management conferences I continuously expressed the opinion, 'Only when our customers are satisfied can we succeed.'

Peter, however, didn't have any in-depth experience of the behaviour of mass customer groups. Instead, he would, with his high level of personal confidence, throw in comments based on day to day involvement with the chattering classes from which he took his views.

He supported them with superficial press comment and the occasional poll usually based on a small sample of say 1,000 people. There are serious dangers in using a sample of 1,000 people to assess the behaviour and needs of a million customers. There's a lot more to it than that, and that kind of simplification trivialises the importance of the customer and how best they can be served. The attitude was not dissimilar to that of the NatWest Board. Very seldom was the customer there considered a significant and important individual in the business. Many lofty views were expressed as to how the business should be run but seldom were they presented from the customer's perspective. There was no realization that satisfied customers bring large and substantial profits. I think there can be little doubt that a long stint in a large retail company is probably a good way to understand how customers feel in large groups.

Peter was to play a central role in the change in management at United Utilities and it was my assumption quite early on that his motive was to gain the Chairmanship of the company. He had, according to the press, been in some sort of competitive arrangement to obtain the Chairmanship of Barclays some years previously, so it would be natural for him still to harbour ambitions to become Chairman of a large public company. In the middle of 1997 there was a great deal of aggressive dialogue between some of the non-Executive Directors and Brian Staples over the issue of remuneration for the Executives. This led to the resignation of one of the non-Executive Directors, subsequently withdrawn, and a general debate about relationships between the Chief Executive and the Board, and myself for that matter. Peter led the discussion in late June.

About the middle of June the non-Executives and I met to discuss this difficulty in the relationships between the Chief Executive and the rest of the Board. Peter led the discussion; I stayed silent. At the end of the discussion all unanimously wanted the removal of the Chief Executive and I accepted their view. The general notion that I made this decision is quite untrue. I stayed silent during the debate but concurred with the conclusion once it was made. There was no way back. All the non-Executives had lost confidence for one reason or another in the Chief Executive. I further took the view, in the interests of the company, that we should act quickly and that we should carry out this change of office before the Annual General Meeting which took place at the end of July so as not to mislead the shareholders at the AGM. I got from the Board very little support from that point onwards.

Involved in all this, with great dignity and total integrity, were the two principals of our merchant bank Kleinwort Benson but the same could not be said for our principal broker, NatWest. The situation was difficult enough for the organization to seek Brian's removal. I wanted Peter Middleton to be present at the exit interview, but in the event, he could not, which came as no surprise, as he was frequently not able to attend key meetings, and in our prior discussions with our advisers, the NatWest adviser tipped off Brian Staples as to what was going to happen. This caused confusion and mayhem, doing enormous damage to the companies.

I believe I was let down by Peter Middleton, and Jane Newell, a relatively new Board member. After the AGM Robert Norbury, NatWest, suggested to Peter Middleton and Eric Clark that they sent a round robin to the principal investors. He was not specific about the subject, but I disagreed. The next step was for all advisers to meet on Wednesday 6 August to draw up plans and seek the Board's directions. On Monday 4 August Robert Norbury sent a letter by fax which seemed to indicate I had agreed to a proposal though I had not.

Bob Furguson, the Company Finance Director, called Norbury to check that no meetings had been arranged; Norbury returned next day, confirming this. On Wednesday 6 August Peter Middleton called me to complain that he had called my office on Monday night at 5.00 p.m. but had received no response. This was not true. My secretary had received the call and had advised I was not contactable as I was travelling to London, and he had left no message.

In the same conversation I told him I was going to the meeting with advisers to revise communications with investors. He did not mention that he and Jane Newell had already met some of them.

Fifteen minutes later, at the advisers' meeting, it became clear Newell and Middleton had already had meetings with some investors. Our senior banking adviser spoke, suggesting it was inappropriate to have such meetings without the Chairman knowing let alone not being present.

Middleton and Newell met investors without Board approval and without confirmation or discussion of the desirability of such meetings.

What mistakes did I make? Clearly recommending Middleton and Newell to be appointed directors was one. I should have followed Eric Clark's advice not to appoint another Chief Executive and assumed more responsibility myself. Lastly I should have made it clear that it was the non-Executives that wanted the Chief Executive removed and not carried the responsibility myself; but how was I to know that Middleton and Newell would withhold that information from the investors when they met them?

In the middle of all this Peter said that he did not wish to seek my position. I didn't believe him. It was a sad end to what was really a promising opportunity for the Company. The multi-utility process was now possibly misunderstood by the Board and by the remaining executives because United Utilities in effect was demerged and few of the customer or financial benefits seem to have come from that merger, which was financially supported by the shareholders.

It is interesting for me to consider my relationships with my many colleagues in the five major enterprises I have been privileged to work for. I always conducted my personal life separately from my business life and found it difficult to be a manager during working hours while carrying on a different sort of relationship as a friend and confidant outside business. I made this decision very early in my career when, in effect, I stopped going to the pub at night with 'the boys', because I found it somewhat difficult to strike up a different tone the following day. I even felt somewhat compromised by discussions the night before. It's a decision I commend to any young person setting out on a management career. You have to get used to the idea that it is a lonely existence. You have to be able to operate in a self-sufficient way to have any hope of making progress up the career chain. That, of course, does not mean that I didn't have associates who liked me or vice versa. I tried to behave in a professional capacity with everybody as colleagues. It wasn't always possible but I'd like to think that most of the time I achieved it. You tend to find that you don't actually know who are your friends and who are enemies.

I have put this in the book at this point because I really think there were only two serious detractors in my career. Both came later on. If there were others that I had issues with, or difficulties with, or lost arguments or situations to, I put the situation down to business politics, or people having personal convictions which were different from mine. No doubt quite often they were right and I was wrong. But I do not look upon my relationship with Peter Middleton and Betty Grantchester in that light. I saw them as two distinct personal detractors, who clearly didn't like me for one reason or another, and who were both of a mind to prejudice, if not damage, my own position or even character.

It is a strange thing that even where people come from different origins there can sometimes be a correlation between them. That was the case with Betty Grantchester and Peter Middleton. They had similar personal characteristics. They said only what they wanted people to know and withheld, quite often, much of their reasoning and thinking. Their response to directness was abruptness in Peter's case and a feigned coyness in Betty's, to avoid the particular point raised or question asked.

You never really know what's under the surface in relationships anyway, but particularly in business they can get exceptionally complicated.

CHAPTER 9

Other Activities

The Merseyside Development Corporation

THE MERSEYSIDE DEVELOPMENT CORPORATION was set up by statute in 1981 about the time, but not as a consequence, of the Toxteth riots in Liverpool. The initiative was Michael Heseltine's, who believed that development corporations were necessary in certain areas to attract inward investment and to manage the inner parts of the inner cities with special Government financial assistance in a way that wasn't practical through the local Government mechanism.

In the case of the Merseyside Development Corporation, it was essentially the south derelict docks which were designated but later, in 1989, by a separate act a larger area was brought into the jurisdiction of the designated area of the Corporation.

This principally involved the central river locality, a very large area to the north side of Liverpool including the operating docks; central Birkenhead with the large Cammell Laird shipyard and up to the

150

Successful two-week trip to USA to drum up investment in Merseyside.
Left: Harry Rimmer, Leader Liverpool City Council; Right: The late George
Clark, Leader Wirral Council

Wallasey Docks; and a special designated area of New Brighton town itself.

I was appointed the chairman of the Merseyside Development Corporation in April 1991 and served for seven years and three months until the Corporation was disbanded between March and June 1998.

At the time of my appointment the Corporation was suffering, perhaps unfairly, an amount of criticism as the lack of money or investment had not produced results, and in the substantially new designated area it had not really had sufficient time to show progress.

Quite early on we appointed a new Chief Executive who had experience with London Docklands, and set about the regeneration process.

The five main areas – New Brighton, Birkenhead, North, South and Central Liverpool – had detailed designated development plans. We embarked upon a list of compulsory purchase orders so the Corporation could undertake the plans it had identified specifically and individually for those areas.

A programme of attracting clerical jobs in particular from Government organizations had gone well, and was now achieving results. The VAT office was to be removed from Southend to Merseyside where the cost of operation was substantially lower. In reality this did not fully happen as the journey and economic circumstances would have enforced excessive hardship in Southend, but a fair degree of additional work was created in the MDC area for the VAT building. The Child Support Agency based one of its main offices in Birkenhead, the Land Registry Office created a substantial activity and the Treasury, or more particularly the Inland Revenue, occupied an important facility.

South of Liverpool had been the earliest part of the area developed and had been dominated by the 1981 Garden Festival, which went a long way to re-laying the infrastructure and reclaiming a substantial amount of derelict land. The remains of the Festival were turned into a medium sized theme park which continued under new ownership. Much of the rest of the area was turned over to moderately priced but attractive private housing and indeed the Corporation had succeeded in helping to build over 4,500 houses. This completely changed the character of the area.

Further down south Liverpool, Brunswick Park was a new industrial development and business park, which attracted a large number of small enterprises, at least two of which grew quite substantially and moved to other major sites in the Merseyside area.

The Pier Head or central Liverpool was completely re-laid and became an attractive meeting place for people. The Albert Dock scheme, which had been the focal point of the first phase of the Corporation's regeneration, was completed together with the Maritime Museum, a shopping arcade and a Tate of the North Gallery. This was attracting millions of people, over six million one year, visiting the various attractions there.

Visit by Michael Portillo as Minister of Environment to review progress of Merseyside Development Corporation, 1991.

In North Liverpool another major dock area has been cleaned and cleared up and is owned by the Mersey Docks and Harbour Company. A development project of offices and hotels is in train, which again will improve the economic value of the area and complete the regeneration.

A major road system through north Liverpool, which would normally be the responsibility of the Department of Transport and which for technical reasons they could not undertake, has been transformed by the Merseyside Development Corporation. It is known as Atlantic Boulevard, providing pleasant and easy access to small industrial units, the largest of which is Sandhills. Started in 1982 it is now progressively filling up with American and Irish manufacturing interests who wish to start testing the UK as a place to expand their business.

In this area is the Eldonian complex, driven by a magnificent public-spirited individual named Tony McGann who with help particularly from Merseyside Development Corporation, has developed a complex with a village hall, a sports complex, individually chosen houses and a special centre for the elderly relatives of people living in the houses to be near their families and yet not live on top of them. The Eldonian Village is probably the best example of an urban village in the UK.

Further down other houses were developed with a housing association and with private developers. The whole of the canal region was regenerated and revitalized; indeed the whole area is becoming what we wanted – a decent place for people to live and consequently for people to work.

Liverpool was decimated firstly by the take-over of many of its companies and therefore the removal of its decision making base, and secondly by the inept decision of Governments, in the 1950s, to move people out to new towns, thus depriving the city of its population. A low population means no economy or little economy and we did much to reverse that process by bringing people back.

On the Birkenhead side Hamilton Square's magnificent Victorian buildings were renovated and attracted back new professional businesses.

Going down the river towards Cammell Laird, more new pleasant houses were built. When Cammell Laird became vacant after VSEL pulled out after making the last ships there, support and help in financial and planning terms were given to the 800, possibly more, jobs on automotive products and ship repair activities.

To the north is the Twelve Quays site on which a substantial start has been made, a technology park with the principal support of John Moores University, the polytechnic as it was in Liverpool, and plans are afoot for a roll-on-roll-off ferry for Irish traffic.

In New Brighton the main street has been re-laid, reorganized and redeveloped. Much housing has been built. A large vacant recreational site has been the subject of interest by a major American destination hotel which has so far been frustrated by the leisure laws of Britain which can be restrictive in terms of the menu of entertainment that can be offered in one establishment.

During its lifetime the Corporation has produced in the region of

25,000 new jobs; it has brought in probably £900 million new investment privately; it has built over 4,500 houses; it has reclaimed much land and built much carriageway and pathway. Everybody agrees it has changed the whole nature, character and economy of central Merseyside.

The Corporation itself finished in 1998. It had run its course. There is still much to be done but it has laid strong foundations to ensure that this is possible.

I found my seven years with Merseyside Development Corporation a most interesting experience. I gained a complete insight, without reservation, into the formal workings of Government and relationships with civil servants and Ministers. In particular I saw a variety of Ministers responsible for the Corporation during that period, and a number of Permanent Secretaries and senior civil servants. They always treated me in a formal way, which I feel comfortable with, and whilst some of the discussions were long and tedious there was much wisdom in the approach that they applied.

MDC had its critics. One was Rex Makin, a local solicitor who had a column in the *Liverpool Echo*. Rex is very close to the Liberal Party then in opposition. He made no secret of his dislike of me and other volunteers who worked to improve the economic and cultural conditions on Merseyside. I at MDC and others such as the Chairman of the Royal Liverpool Philarmonic Orchestra were frequently the butt of his rather perverse sarcastic articles in the *Liverpool Echo*. It was not helpful to our efforts.

Another critic was Peter Kilfoyle, the Labour MP for the area, who, it was suggested, was friendly with Rex Makin. I don't know if this was so or not, but they both shared the same attitude towards the Corporation. When New Labour were elected in May 1997 they effected decisions which very quickly had economic reversals for Liverpool and Merseyside. In one of those Peter Kilfoyle was to play a part.

The most attractive site on Merseyside is Kings Dock, adjacent to Albert Dock and overlooking the river. In the early 1990s Kings Dock suffered a serious planning blight. This had arisen because the development proposals at the time had been criticised quite ferociously by the Royal Fine Arts Commission, English Heritage and other organizations whose responsibility is to maintain proper heritage standards on key sites and buildings in Britain. This blight hung over the site until MDC commissioned Sir Richard Rogers to design a master plan, which in turn was discussed extensively with the then Secretary of State for the Environment. We took the view that it would not proceed until it was endorsed by the Secretary of State, as it was unreasonable to expect a developer to undertake the work, the cost, and the disappointment involved in developing a project which might be subsequently torpedoed at the planning stage. The master plan, following full consultation with the key groups, was duly approved by the Secretary of State, and we marched forward confident in the fact that now the task of finding a developer and the right development was what was needed to develop that magnificent site.

Eddie Healey, who runs the Stadium Group which has built major shopping centres in Düsseldorf and Sheffield, came forward with a £100 million investment programme, without seeking a pound of MDC or Government support, to put on the site a mixture of retail, culture and entertainment facilities, fitting into the stringent requirements of the Richard Rogers Master Plan. MDC set up a sub-group of directors and consultants to examine what was best for the site. Quite apart from the Healey proposal, other suggestions were studied. All wanted substantial public funds. Some were demonstrably not viable. The Kings Dock site was considered extensively as to the economics, Government funding and planning to come up with the right solution which would create jobs for thousands and increase activity in Central Liverpool.

The Eddie Healey proposal met all the requirements. It went through the Planning Committee. All interested parties were fully consulted and the application received planning approval with no dissension or objection whatsoever. Shortly after that the Government changed and it became apparent, from the copy of the letter that we saw, that Peter Kilfoyle had written to the new Environment Minister raising issues which showed a preference for a different use for the site. To everybody's astonishment the Minister called in the planning approval and instigated a Public Enquiry. In one stroke he wiped out £100 million of commercial investment in Liverpool, together with the associated jobs. The developer wouldn't wait for the result of the Public Enquiry and withdrew. Not a brick has been laid on the site years later.

The second major setback was with talks we had been having for some time with a company in America who wanted to build a Las Vegas-type destination hotel at New Brighton. They were discussing an $800 million investment, with no public funding, and were very enthusiastic. Many of the local groups were interested in this even though they were sceptical about the concept of gambling. The only thing which appeared to be standing in the way of what would appear to be vested interests was that that kind of activity in Britain requires a membership registration of 48 hours, which was reduced to 24 hours, before a person is allowed entrance. That would not have worked because people might have travelled up to 200 miles to spend a day or possibly a night at that establishment, and therefore membership would have to be instant, subject to identification. Those archaic rules which now act as a substantial protection for existing casino operators were hard to justify against the background of the National Lottery, which allows any sixteen-year-old entrance to any place where they can buy lottery tickets and scratch cards to spend any amount of money they wish.

An investment of that size in Merseyside, which would have brought between 7,000 and 10,000 jobs in an area desperately needing them, was not one that you would think a new Government would lightly dismiss. George Howarth, one of the Ministers at the Home Office, wrote a letter to the effect that the Government weren't prepared to consider an amendment to the Gaming Act, regardless of the fact that in his own area he could see the prospect for substantial employment. He should not have handled that decision, but should have got another Minister to deal with it. Apart from anything else he is already being severely criticised for his comments on the Hillsborough disaster which have caused a great deal of emotion in the local community. The Government indicates now that it might scrap the requirement for prior membership.

John Prescott diminished the prospects of Liverpool Airport becoming a effective large scale facility by approving its sale to a private sector operator. Whilst well meaning, this denied substantial funds to achieve the kind of airport dimension that Liverpool could support in the area. Because Merseyside's per capita income was below a certain standard set by the EEC, the area was designated as an Objective One region, and as a result had received almost £600 million funds from Europe.

The new Government was somewhat surprised when the Labour Party in Liverpool lost the local elections, and set up an enquiry to find out what caused this. I should think the reason for their reduced popularity is pretty obvious from the catalogue of decision errors which are described above.

I would like to think that at Merseyside Development Corporation I made some very good friends. It was a Board that all our members enjoyed being on.

Chris Farrow joined Merseyside Development Corporation in the latter part of 1990, having held a senior position with the London Docklands Development Corporation, with particular responsibility for the Surrey Docks, where he had effectively been the Chief Executive of the London Docklands Development Corporation's regeneration programme.

Chris is one of those people who never really gets the recognition and reward to which he is entitled. To be the Chief Executive of the Merseyside Development Corporation, which is what the Government call a 'Non-Departmental Public Body', means that in all respects he is part of the Department, in this case the Department of the Environment, but he is treated in certain respects differently from the staff in that Department. What that really means is that a Chief

Executive has full liability and accountability as if he were a civil servant, but does not receive the payment or the recognition he would have had in the private sector. The task of being Chief Executive of an Urban Development Corporation, an environmental and economic regenerating activity, requires him to be a jack of many trades. It is difficult to describe all of them, but the fundamental requirements of financial management; people management; business planning; competent administration; understanding of construction road planning; infrastructure planning, building design, the work of surveyors and architects and the workings of Local Government, are some but not all of the skills and experience that a Chief Executive of an Urban Development Corporation needs.

We were very fortunate in being able to recruit Chris because he had acquired many of these skills in his management of Surrey Docks. He was a very good man manager and was able to double the productivity of the existing staff within five years of being in the job. To achieve a 15 per cent per annum increase in productivity is a management achievement that few ever aspire to. Additionally he was able to change the mental outlook of the entire staff by motivating them and communicating with them in a way which would have taken him to a senior position had he been in a normal commercial business organization.

If I have one quarrel at all with civil servants, it is the way in which they look upon people like Chris. They never particularly like the idea of them being other than a rank in a certain category position in the Civil Service hierarchy. But his skills are far more commercial and he has considerable commercial value. There were numerous difficulties in getting what the Board collectively believed was a more adequate remuneration than he received during his service with the Corporation. Of course that was important to Chris, but it wasn't his prime motive, which was his work and his endeavours to see the regeneration of the area. This he achieved and it must have given him and the many people who could see it, a lot of satisfaction. He endured much unfair criticism of the political kind, from the MPs for Liverpool in particular.

He did a great job for Liverpool. Perhaps one day this will be properly recognized. Certainly if there's anything that can be said to be a driving force behind Chris it is his ability to take the local people with him while being a Cockney in Merseyside. That does not happen very often. It's not a place that easily accepts strangers, and particularly not from London, and yet he was able to achieve full acceptance in his time there.

From local Government we had Harry Rimmer, Leader of Liverpool Council, who did much to remove political militancy. He was replaced as Leader of Liverpool by Frank Prendergast who carried on the work after him, a devoted citizen struggling with the difficult problems of the City of Liverpool itself. From across the water in the Wirral was the Leader, David Jackson. All of them, together with a representative from Sefton Borough Council, worked enthusiastically with the Corporation and vice versa for the economic regeneration of the region. There was no bad feeling with the local Government people, although there may have been with local MPs, who felt left out. The formation of the Urban Development Corporations was a central Government initiative and was bound to affect and offend some people, but the results proved the value of having the Corporation.

From the private sector came Muriel Downs. She was a very successful business lady, who was the Managing Director of a company that made bath fittings, in particular a variety of shower cubicles which, I believe, were quite a significant market leader. Muriel was also very active in the Confederation of British Industry in the region. Indeed she brought much business acumen to the Board debate. She left a little earlier than the remaining members, who all departed when the Merseyside Development Corporation finally ceased to exist at the end of June 1998, as she wished to take up a position in which she had an equity interest and I have no doubt that she did very well in that venture.

Then there was Michael Parkinson, an expert in economic regeneration, and Paula Ridley, a person very dedicated to public service, on the subject of Arts and Housing Development in particular.

Paula had some rather strict views on political correctness which I didn't actually adhere to, and from time to time I was chastized accordingly. It was a warm but formal relationship that we had. There was Geoff Prince, the ex Chief Executive of the Royal Insurance Company; John Handley, an expert on environmental matters; Ted McGonagle, an ex NatWest Regional Director; and Eric Clark to whom I alluded earlier, who had also been invited to join the United Utilities Board. I had a great admiration for his huge intellect which he would apply specifically in a highly logical way to solve problems. Unlike some intellects he had no arrogance with it, but sometimes people found him difficult to comprehend because of his reasoning and his simplicity of approach. He never lost patience but basically tried to get his point of view across and invariably it won the day.

Lastly was a character who was larger than life, Clive Lewis. He was President of the Royal Institute of Chartered Surveyors one year, and was senior partner of a major firm of Chartered Surveyors in London. He was invaluable in terms of bringing to the Board property opportunities and was in effect our representative in London.

I'd like to think that I made some good friends on this Board. It was certainly a most enjoyable experience.

The Mersey Barrage

My next major project was as Chairman of the Mersey Barrage Company. This idea was initiated many years ago and some studies were carried out by the Merseyside County Council, which was dissolved in 1984 or thereabouts. The River Mersey has the second highest tidal regime in the world after the Bay of Fundy and has a 30ft spring tide. The idea of building a barrage across the river to capture that water on the ingoing tide and use it to generate power when the tide ebbed was the principle behind the whole project.

It would cost close on £1 billion to build but have very low operating costs and would under the conventional pricing regime of the time be competitive once in operation. The real problem was raising all the cash at the beginning to build the barrage itself.

I was able to form a Board of the senior local business people, including Trevor Furlong of Mersey Docks & Harbour Co. and Brian Thaxter from Barclays Bank. Others were Directors from Rolls Royce, NEI, Tarmac, Costains and a couple of eminent politicians, Sir Peter Morrison and Alastair Goodlad.

By raising money from twenty or so shareholders, all of whom were big companies, and having those funds matched by Government funds, we completed the entire pre-design study and concept study, modelling and drilling the river basin for tests on the sub-strata.

There were a number of possible locations for the barrage and a large test model was created at the National Hydraulic Laboratories which gave a live model test of the whole scheme. We were able by and large to placate most of the objectors with the exception possibly of the bird lobby.

The Government set aside £1 billion for non-fossil fuel levy. We needed £400 million as a loan, because of the special problem of having to finance the construction and having no income until the barrage started to generate power.

There was a great deal of interest in this project by all Secretaries of State for Energy: Peter Walker, Cecil Parkinson, John Wakeham and subsequently, when the Department of Energy became part of the Department of Trade & Industry, from Tim Eggar, the Minister responsible, and partly from Michael Heseltine.

I think we would have got the money if it hadn't been for the sudden change in the price structure of the basic fuels of oil and coal and the horrendous demise of the coal industry. It became politically obvious that it was not possible to support, even by a lower non-fossil fuel levy, a project of such significance during a time of falling fuel costs and massive redundancies in the conventional fuel industry such as coal.

The works were put in abeyance. The company still exists and one day, you never know, all that hard work and effort could be rewarded and the project may arise like the phoenix, not from the fire but from the river.

SHADO

The next organization I was involved in was SHADO. This stands for the Self Help Against Drugs Organization, administered by a totally dedicated lady named Ann Milling. It is run on a shoe-string, in some cases with very little help from local politicians and others with active hindrance from them. Kenneth Baker was the President of SHADO and I helped and assisted him, principally on walks and other limited activities, to raise something in the region of £450,000 for this small charity.

SHADO was unique in the sense that the parents of the addicts met and, by self help amongst a group, were able sometimes to find cures for their children, most of whom were adolescents.

Working or being with these unfortunate people is a disturbing experience because really it is a social problem. It is not so much addiction to drugs but the need to be part of the crowd, which drives so many of these young people to stay as drug addicts, which gets out of control and destroys their lives.

The pattern of drug addiction stems from the lack of a job and the person's position of being part of the crowd on the street. It is

Raising funds for SHADO, Ann Milling between the author and Ken Baker.

particularly hard for girls as their boyfriends expect them to behave as they do. A special difficulty for boys is that if they withdraw from being part of the group, they are effectively confined to home all the time as there is nothing else to do.

I am told that one in three of these groups that visited SHADO successfully stopped their adolescent children from taking drugs. We don't know. What little we did I hope was of some help, but it illustrated to me the vast problem facing probably the whole of Britain, not just Liverpool, and the inadequacy of any effective way of tackling it.

Alder Hey Children's Hospital

I next became involved with the Alder Hey Anniversary Children's Appeal Fund. The aim was to raise money to fund an advanced cancer treatment. Paul McCartney was the President, but because of the pressures of his work was unable to spend much time on it. I was asked to be its Vice-President to help arrange the funding. Jimmy Tarbuck and Ken Dodd came in and Jimmy Tarbuck became the Vice-President for the entertainment section which was organized by way of golf events. We did raise the money for the appeal, particularly through the effort of the three lady executives who ran it.

I greatly admired the work of Jimmy and Ken and of their colleagues, Stan Boardman and others, and the support they gave to this wonderful scheme. I was deeply touched when, some years later, the children from the wards which had been built sent me a special birthday card written and produced by them. This was to induce me to chair a second appeal to build a new Children's Oncology Unit which will be opened in the second quarter of 2003.

Everton Football Club

As I mentioned in my comments on Littlewoods I frequently went to football matches with Sir John, who was the largest shareholder in both Liverpool Football Club and Everton Football Club, and was until his death, by exception, allowed to be so. Football Association regulations prevented one person from owning more than a nominal financial interest in a second club. Sir John and I used to talk about the Everton football matches and he would relay his views, really our views, to the then Chairman and frequently asked me to join the Board. I think he had in mind that he would like me to be its Chairman. He really saw Everton as an extension of the Littlewoods business. I, for my part, continually refused this because I thought it would detract from my ability to handle the burdens of the job at Littlewoods.

Unbeknown to me Sir John agreed that I be appointed to the Board and presented it to me as an accomplished fact rather than a further request by him. He didn't like being refused and therefore had acted unilaterally on the matter.

Everton became for me a symbol of what was happening in Liverpool: a club that was struggling to regain, on a consistent basis, the highest standard in the playing order of football competition. I saw my position simply as a businessman and I looked at it totally as a company. Over the ten years we had some dramatic changes, one of which took place when Peter Johnson took over as the principal owner and shareholder of the Club in 1994. Peter did not resolve the difficulties that the club has constantly faced. My formula for success for the Club is the same as for a successful business. It has to be run on a business basis.

Peter was a highly successful businessman in his own company. However, he did not communicate well with the Board and really liked running his own show. This led to a variety of managerial changes, which in themselves were unhelpful, and a lack of effective use of the capital put into the business. Maybe it's too short a time to form that view and maybe I'm wrong and time will tell, but ten years on the Board seemed long enough, our views were becoming different and I felt it was time for me to leave. Of course, I continue to be a fan of the Club.

National Westminster Bank
I had two stints on the Boards of NatWest, the first on the Advisory Board, which was a collection of individuals, mostly customers, who helped advise the Bank and its North West Executives on how to

*William Crowe, American Ambassador, visit to Goodison Park, Everton. Right:
Prof. Fred Nurbury, previously Acting Vice Chancellor, Liverpool University.*

improve its business and customer service. This was an interesting
experience, because I spent time meeting managers and having a
general discussion, but after four years the need for this Board did not
seem to exist and it was disbanded. I subsequently joined the main
board of NatWest. I found the world of banking interesting and was
watching a similar process to that which had taken place in some of the
companies I had run. It was going through a change management
process, against a background of history and legacies of the past which
had to be converted into more contemporary business. This change was
fundamentally technology driven, as with its major competitors in the
field. Working with the Bank was an unusual experience. I would
commend it to all businessmen, because it is helpful in conducting
one's own affairs. I'm not so sure I would recommend it as a career.

The Royal Liverpool Philharmonic
My last endeavour was with the Royal Liverpool Philharmonic Society.
The RLPO is the only orchestra to own its own hall, which had fallen

into serious dilapidation. To help us raise business interest in the Merseyside Development Corporation area they sponsored the RLPO during a tour of the United States. They had been part of the Grand Regatta Concert for which the King of Spain visited Liverpool to celebrate the 500th anniversary of Christopher Columbus's discovery of America.

The concert was magnificent in terms of the international artists who appeared there. There was however controversy arising from it, stirred up principally by local MPs who were against the concept of the Merseyside Development Corporation undertaking such a venture.

The pros and cons notwithstanding, the £17.5 million the concert and the regattas brought to Liverpool by way of revenue was very helpful to the City. Of course the £4.5 million that the Exchequer got by way of taxes far exceeded any costs that Merseyside Development Corporation may have incurred.

Be that as it may, the RLPO, being one of the oldest philharmonic societies in the world, is an artistic jewel in Liverpool, together with its eight or so major museums and art galleries.

I was Chairman of the committee to raise £10 million to rebuild the hall. It was a very satisfying task and we had substantial help from the Government by City Challenge grants, Europe in terms of European grants, Peter Moores as an individual, Littlewoods as a company, and from the other major Liverpool companies. Lastly, a large chunk of the money came from a substantial number of small donations from the Liverpool public.

The money was raised, and in a remarkably short period of time the hall was completed. It really is a monument to what Government, local businesses and individuals can do to reinstate a very fine piece of Art Deco used for a very worthy purpose, the home of the RLPO.

I have been involved in many other smaller activities. However I don't wish this to be a catalogue but simply to illustrate how being in business gives you the chance to play an important role in the local community, if you so wish and put the time in.

CHAPTER 10

They're All Fat Cats Now

I DIDN'T LIKE BEING CALLED a fat cat because of the associations it had, namely somebody taking advantage of a situation to live excessively in a position that was actually yielding no benefit to society. This was simply not true. The salary I took on leaving Littlewoods to join United Utilities dropped by 50 per cent, so I certainly did not take that position for financial reasons. The job itself was by any standards demanding and difficult. There had been years of very low investment. The Chancellor had always put the water industry quite low in his priorities and the industry had for years been underfunded by the Treasury. The infrastructure was simply not there in the case of sewage and waste water. The waste was dumped in the most inappropriate places, mostly in rivers and streams, and heavily polluted the water environment as well as indirectly the land because of the cycle of treatment of the waste water. North West Water had to find funding from the market to undertake this massive investment programme. It took enormous organization and skill to design, construct, supervise and commission the many plants that had to be built in this early period of privatization. Extraordinary personnel training schemes were needed to get some efficiency into the business, which by and large hadn't changed for many decades. It was a difficult transition for the employees. A massive design and construction investment programme was needed to raise the capital to undertake the work required, and it was necessary to give the company some balance so that in the future we would have substantial income other than simply from the citizens of the North West.

We embarked on extensive overseas investment, operating a programme which would bring both jobs and capital back into the UK over a period of time. It was by no means a simple task. On the contrary it was very difficult, and it wasn't made any easier by the fact that the Press never seemed to recognize any of these fundamental major activities that were taking place. They went on incessantly about Fat Cats and price increases. They ignored the fact that increases were necessary, not only to raise some of the income for this capital investment programme but also simply to bring the cost of UK water into line with, but not up to, European costs. Over and above that was the failure of the accountancy profession to describe what profit really is, i.e. the principal and main source of cash supply for investment; it of course pays dividends to shareholders and pays interest to lenders. But interest to lenders and dividends to shareholders are quite simply the same sort of repayment except that the shareholders take a substantial risk and are therefore bound to demand higher returns than a risk-free bank loan.

I was in the wrong place at the wrong time. I think I've dealt with that before in the chapter on United Utilities. Some people took advantage of the press comment and made much of it for their own selfish political gains. It doesn't matter now. I probably feel a lot more at home being a 'Fat Cat' because whichever way you look at it they're all Fat Cats now. It was started by people who at that stage were running a campaign using this type of remark. I mean of course the present Government, which was then in opposition. The Prime Minister's salary in 1997 was £102,000, but is now £163,000 a year, a 60 per cent increase over four years. That's not bad going. Likewise Cabinet Ministers receive £118,000 a year, as opposed to £87,000 in 1997 – a 35 per cent increase. That's not bad either. That would have attracted a great deal of criticism if it had taken place in my time as Chairman of United Utilities. There the basic salary I received, although high, rose very slowly while I was there, save for the time when I forwent the bonus which was included towards the end of the period. MPs themselves, according to the *Daily Mail* on 5 July 2001, had voted themselves a £31,000 increase in pay and perks. Some MPs from the left and right opposed this on the grounds that they were setting the wrong example.

Ian McCartney was one of the Ministers involved in this enormous increase in Ministers' pay. He was upset when at the largest fringe gathering of the Labour Party 2001 Conference he was jeered at and branded by the people present as a 'weasel', because in spite of the enormous salary increase that he and his colleagues had enjoyed, he was not able to find ways of increasing the incomes of pensioners. 'I don't deserve this,' he said, 'I'm not a weasel, I come from a Trade Union movement,' as if somehow or other that would satisfy the three hundred or so people who were angry that he was getting more than they had any prospect of enjoying.

There were also grounds for suggesting the politicians didn't deserve any pay rise. Business people, whatever their level of remuneration, do not get increases if they fail during the course of their performance. There have been some instances recently of people who get paid sums when they get sacked, but that's the nature of the contracts which were negotiated when people wanted their services. For my part I would like to see substantial rewards for success but no compensation for failure. At least 50 per cent of executives lose their jobs because of style: that hard to define personal quality which is probably the driving force behind the success of a business, but which, because of jealousy or other human frailties, people don't particularly like. I don't think it really matters. If a Chief Executive is succeeding financially then that's the important factor and there seems no good reason at all to remove him from his position simply because people don't like his personality.

Going back to the politicians – they're working shorter hours than they did in the past; they've got limits on their day; very seldom do they have long meetings. Most of the time many of them aren't in the House anyway because of the majority position of the Labour Party in the new Government. Their performance on such things as the National Health Service, transport and education has been well documented as falling far short of what it should be, let alone what they promised it would be when they were elected in 1997. They seem desperately short of any political initiatives and fondly imagine the solution to all things is in their ability to manage it and throw endless resources at these problems in the self delusion that that will cure it. It won't. Without a different political approach to the National Health Service or schools or other major institutions, without a political initiative everything will stay the same. You cannot manage organizations as large as the National Health Service with a work force of 1.2 million people by a Secretary of State who believes he can make all of the decisions. It's the kind of situation that no middle manager would ever even contemplate because management know the limits to what they can actually manage. Politicians very seldom make managers, any more than managers make politicians. So there is a reasonable case for saying, 'Why do they award themselves all this money?' They spend less time at work. They show little sign of progress. They are completely bereft of any serious political initiatives, the life blood of any successful thriving political system.

One of the concerns is the way politicians feel they should be treated differently, for instance on the question of benefits in kind. Professional and Executive employees are taxed on benefits in kind because they are seen as another form of income. The question of benefits in kind enjoyed by politicians came to a head when people criticised the money Ministers were authorising for expenditure on their own residences. The case for this in some instances was also open to question since their normal business is conducted on office premises. In particular they illustrated this unfair view when they refused to accept that there is no benefit in kind to executives who really have to split their time between two locations and consequently do need two homes, even though they only live in one of them as a residence. Tax in Britain has been increasingly levied at a higher rate on this so-called benefit of a second home if it is provided by the company, to the point that tax of 8 per cent of the capital on the value of the premises is levied. This is a very high figure for the same benefit that Ministers enjoy and for which they do not pay a penny and show no inclination to do so. However, when this became a topical issue they agreed to pay a proportion of the tax on improvements and renovations carried out during or prior to their tenure for which they enjoyed the benefit. But they were not at all straightforward on this and you will find that in the end they inveigle this down to an almost meaningless figure they will be required to pay.

The Paymaster General to the Treasury, in a written answer to the Commons, ruled that the work was taxable. 'Where refurbishments to accommodation consist of repairs, decorations or furniture, tax is charged on the benefit,' she said. The Treasury however admitted that Ministers are being charged only minor sums, compared with the value of the work, because it is claimed that their official homes are necessary for them to carry out their official duties. Because of this ruling Ministers pay tax on refurbishment to a maximum of one tenth of their ministerial salary. The £49,822 they get as an MP is not taken into account, reducing the bill further. As they are all on the higher rate of 40 per cent they are paying just 4 per cent of ministerial salary. All other employees have to pay tax at rates up to 40 per cent. The Chancellor was simply addressing the cost of the repairs, not the capital value of the accommodation. It's a pretty useful benefit in kind in consideration of the minimal taxation which is imposed.

But are they performing? There are various views on this, of course, but I think it is generally accepted that the most important aspect of the public domain which needs resolving is the inadequacy of the National Health Service. I don't think anyone would think the Government are performing in that area. They are actually encouraging a weakening of performance, if that is possible. This in spite of all the hard work undertaken by the professionals in the service, who labour under the dictates of the enormous bureaucratic machine that has been set up in the Health Service. A fundamental principle of management is that you don't give money to people who are not performing. The easiest excuse in the world when the job isn't being done is, 'I haven't got enough resources.' The task of management is to make the best performance with the resources available. It is not the job of the manager to keep saying, 'I need more resources.' It certainly wouldn't happen in a private company. A non-performing man asking for more investment would certainly get no consideration of his request. Managers have to prove they are able to make things happen, that they are capable of making investment yield some results, and of improving efficiency and performance in the areas under their control. Then and only then would the private sector give them more funds.

That doesn't apply in the public sector. Every time there is a outcry over some incident which is, in human terms, miserable, there is another demand for yet more money. And that is exactly what the Government does. It throws more and more money at problems without the vaguest idea how it is going to get to the grass roots level of the organization and without any measure whatsoever of the value for the money that they are putting into the NHS. Indeed it looks to me, and I have a passing association with the National Health Service, that the more money they put in the more coordinators they appoint. Coordinators are anathema to American management, who always jokingly say that a coordinator keeps two people apart who otherwise would have worked together. The only answer to the National Health Service, or indeed any other organization that is not performing properly, is political, not management. To chop and change your mind is not going to help someone understand what the political decision is. League tables and all sorts of grand statements have been made but not one political initiative. That political initiative would have to be based on the fundamentals of their performance, customer choice and the ability of the management to operate in an unfettered way whilst being wholly accountable. That is, of course, highly possible and you don't even have to get into the public versus private money debate; you simply have to examine the way the hospital services in other countries function. They are not forever clamouring for more money; they function on basic parameters such as cost per bed and turnover rates; and more particularly the local management have influence and the customers have their choice.

The Fat Cat propaganda was a mean trick that this present Government played on certain individuals, particularly those with an extremely good track record over a long period in British industry, simply to take political advantage of the public's lack of understanding of the processes needed in industrial change. I don't think they would get away with it in the public sector because the public have more idea about what's going on and the Unions are very vocal as well. But they should examine their own motives after taking that route to cause demonstration cases of people who were not in a position to answer back, for their own political advantage, and think about their own position *vis-à-vis* the rewards they have now taken in terms of the true 'Fat Cat' salary enhancement situation.

National Lottery

As Littlewoods Pools was part of my responsibility as Chief Executive of Littlewoods, for a long time we advised against the National Lottery and we took basically a high moral stance about the dangers of easy gambling. Nobody of course believed that but nevertheless we tried it with little success. In particular Littlewoods Pools was not a big cash cow as people perceived nor was it a highly profitable organization. It had been run for a long time as a business, principally for the benefit of the public. It didn't hold much cash but what it collected on Saturday it gave out again the following Wednesday. It was a weekly pool. Initially and for quite some time it had been operating some very large charitable organizations, the best known one being the Football Trust. This poured great sums into football before television started to give the clubs plenty of financial input, essentially to improve the quality and safety of their grounds, particularly following the Hillsborough disaster. Most clubs got substantial grants from the Football Trust during that period, and we were consulted in Lord Taylor's deliberations on the issue. He recommended all-seating football grounds which we very much supported and had done for some time. Another is the Sports and Arts Foundation Trust, which is not for football or cricket. I'm not sure how cricket got left out. It is a trust to help other sports with capital programmes and to help fund the arts. All these Trusts worked very well, firstly because Littlewoods played no role in them but simply paid them the money to dispense. Secondly they had highly defined but quite restrictive and narrow terms of reference so it could be explained why some people got money and others were unsuccessful. Thirdly, it never gave money for income and revenue purposes. Quite simply if you do that the day comes when you haven't got any money to dispense. You pull the revenue expenditure, you specifically close down whatever it is you've been supporting and then you get the blame as if it's your fault, with no recognition of the years you've been giving income support.

These Trusts worked well and we made strong representations to the Government that whatever happened it was vital that a National Lottery had similar activities. In the event it did not. The National Lottery had boards dispensing money but they were directly influenced by the Minister for Culture. In other words it became an arm of the Government and in addition to that they also started dispensing money for revenue purposes, particularly to the outreach type of organizations about whose activities the British public know little. It is important because how you spend the money for good causes out of the Lottery directly affects the public's view of the Lottery itself. If they think that money is not going to what they believe are good causes they very quickly lose enthusiasm for the activity. The whole thing was further exacerbated because of such projects as Wembley Stadium and the Dome. Indeed the whole financial outlook on the Lottery for good causes became a hypothetical tax which instead of being dispensed by the Treasury was dispensed by the Minister for Culture. That we advised strongly should not happen. It would be very damaging to the Lottery and indeed it has been just that.

The second thing which is very important about a small bet, long odds lottery, which has an instant attraction when for a pound you can get millions, is that it must be self-sustaining. The moment you announce a lottery of that description you have got a clamour for tickets. A short while afterwards when people haven't won the millions of pounds or indeed won anything at all the enthusiasm drops very rapidly. There are processes and techniques which keep a lottery like that self-sustaining which haven't been even vaguely considered or applied. In a lottery situation you are facing up to the problem of dispensation of funds which is very much disliked by the public. The public simply have no encouragement other than walking into the shop to put their £1 on the Lottery.

The 'Fat Cat' thing also overtook the Lottery. The organisers should have been, and were, paid pretty good salaries for doing such an incredible job getting it up and running. That was a masterpiece and people involved should be heavily congratulated but I think it started to go wrong when bonuses were being paid for non-performance activities. The one in particular was the loyalty bonus, which was set up when Camelot was bidding against Virgin. That was perfectly all right in itself. I mean, the purpose of a loyalty bonus is to ask people to stay until the end of the term that the company is trading. But the fact is that they are also designed so that if the company continues trading at the end of the term, the loyalty bonuses aren't paid, because the employees have been rewarded by keeping their jobs. In this case the bonuses were paid even though Camelot retained the operation of the Lottery, and this was one too many to accept. I think on balance Virgin probably would have done the better job. It would have been different. If you can't have a self sustaining gambling activity and the mechanisms which keep them self sustaining which haven't been applied by the National Lottery then indeed you need to keep on changing the formula on offer.

I could go on forever about this 'Fat Cat' issue, but let's have a look at United Utilities itself. Sir Peter Middleton's salary from 1998 to 2001 went from £40,700 to £150,000, an increase of 150 per cent. That's not bad considering that in my time he used to have to make immense efforts to come and see the business. Now he has got far more outside responsibilities than he had then. Jane Newall went from £25,000 to £45,000, which is somewhat above inflation. The one person who looks as though he's been following his own philosophy is John Seed, going from £24,500 to £35,000. As the Chairman of the Remuneration Committee he must have had the most difficult job.

Well, there it is, there are a lot of other 'Fat Cats' around as well but it is now, as it was in 1997, a boring subject, one easily prone to exaggeration, distortion and aggression. It does no good in any circle of activity to encourage that kind of jealousy and reaction. I do hope we are coming to a period when people recognize the efforts, talents and skills of people in key positions in the country and respect their value to the community as happens in other countries.

CHAPTER 11

My Personal Life

IT HAS BEEN SAID by a friend reading the early draft of this book, that it conveys the impression of a person who keeps everything to himself. That in part is because of the manner in which I'd written it but also because the first draft did not contain a single comment or note about my personal life. It left people with the impression that there was something substantially missing. This was subsequently confirmed to me when I read that interesting book called *Tainted by Experience* by Sir John Drummond, someone of the same age and perhaps similar experience to myself. It struck me that there was no mention at all in the book about his personal life. I kept on thinking about this as I travelled through his extensive and exciting experiences in the music profession.

It may well be true that I do keep my personal feelings to myself. This started in my childhood when, as I described, I was evacuated and people were all strange to me. It carried on through my working life, because it is a fact that in business or industry those who are easy or lax enough to let their feelings become known are quite likely to be the first snapped up by the piranhas in the battles of industry and all the politics that go with it. So I'm sure that by nature I do keep the most intimate things to myself, and I've also found it a good policy in dealing with people. The old expression: 'God protect me from my friends. I can deal with my enemies by myself,' is one I picked up early in life and I'm glad that I did.

So I decided, on reflection, that to give some balance to the book I really had no choice but to delve into my personal life. I have discussed my early years at the start of the book, and I lived a reasonably normal youth and early twenties existence with a number of female friends.

Nothing deadly serious. I was daunted by the prospect of any responsibilities and was progressing quite well with my own philosophy. I reached my mid twenties without getting involved in marriage, as most of my friends had, which was quite the thing in the 50s and 60s.

I met my first wife Patricia when I was about twenty-three and she was about twenty-four. I'd just finished my short stint in the Merchant Navy on the *Empress of France* and her boyfriend was on one of the Cunard passenger ships, which was moored in the next dock to us in Gladstone Dock in Liverpool. I don't quite know what was going on with her boyfriend, but I met her a few weeks later at a Liverpool dance – quite a coincidence really because as I explained later, she came from Runcorn and was seldom in Liverpool, particularly not for Saturday night dances. We had a two to three year courtship involving buying an old car I couldn't afford to keep because the cost of the repairs were so high and finishing up with a 250cc motor bike. So it wasn't exactly a luxurious period. She introduced me to her various friends in Runcorn and subsequently to her vacation locations, generally North Wales and, in particular, Anglesey.

It was a chequered courtship and then I finished up in Switzerland, in 1961, at the age of twenty-six, starting my very interesting and exciting experiences in the computer industry in its embryonic stage, and working with European people as opposed to British. We decided to get married in that year.

The situation didn't really lend itself to an obviously stable marriage. I was certainly unsure of where I'd finish up working and I'm not quite sure she wanted to marry anyone who did not comply with her preconceived idea of the sort of person a girl from ICI should marry.

It was difficult to sort ourselves out when I was already travelling quite a bit, with no real foundation to build on, but it was clear that we certainly weren't going to follow the traditional matrimonial path of a boy from Liverpool and a girl from a northern chemical town.

My sister, three years older than I, got married in July and we got married in August, which imposed a very heavy domestic burden on my father who wasn't used to appearing in the North of England in two successive months. Nevertheless he did and they really were rather special occasions. Family reunions, no doubt, are the same at any wedding but when families live in different parts of England it is nice to have everyone back together if only for a short period of time.

Immediately after the marriage we went to live in Switzerland but in an attempt to get sorted out I came back shortly afterwards to work in Manchester. I didn't particularly like it. I bought a home for a short period of time but found myself back in London very soon in my first management job in the London headquarters. We moved to Surrey and from then onwards for the rest of my life I've frequently had a home both in Surrey or Berkshire and in Cheshire or Lancashire. Pat and I travelled to London every day from Bagshot to the City. This was not a very pleasant experience and certainly not for a young woman. In any event she was approaching thirty and now she wanted to have children.

During her pregnancy Pat was constantly ill. She didn't eat and consequently was very difficult to live with, as I suppose all young mothers are – most young mothers anyway – and the doctor was paying little attention to her. We were convinced there was something unusual, possibly twins, but we didn't get anywhere with the doctor and this situation continued until an unusual occurrence happened in Bagshot. A new doctor arrived straight from the Indian sub-continent. This was 1960 and that was an rare event. I always had an affinity and friendship with people from that region and this was one of a number who have been supportive through my life. The doctor quickly diagnosed that firstly it was a multiple birth and secondly that Pat was was suffering from a very high blood pressure disorder, which was very dangerous in her condition.

From that point onwards she received the best of treatment. Indeed she was in hospital at least two weeks before the expected birth and I became known as a 'hospital husband'. Things were progressing in terms of maternity provision then and women could actually go around the hospital to see what the facilities were like. By God, it must have

Daughters Stephanie and Samantha, 1975.

terrified them: a bit like a nineteenth century workhouse with sombre tiles. In a fortnight my twin daughters were born. Whatever has happened with my marriage, I've always had a close, loving affinity with my daughters. I think it is a testament to my ex-wife and me that my relationship with my daughters has been allowed to continue happily over the last thirty-seven years.

With babies around it was quite an experience for two months. I was deeply involved in major computer projects with the Royal Navy and Royal Air Force at the time. It was a frenetic period back and forth to Bath and Gloucester for the two major contracts. It was an exhausting and difficult time, but it worked out all right and then with increasing mobility and income we moved into a detached house in Camberley. This was on a main road but was comfortable in spite of being very noisy and perhaps somewhat dangerous. During this time I was struggling with the demands of my career. Unless you lived through the 60s as a young person, you'd never be able to explain it to anybody else. There was extraordinary freedom for women. Money was coming through, mostly earned by the husband, but also by the wife. There was a wild social outburst against the background of the Rolling Stones, the

Beatles and all the wonderful musicians at the time, much partying and frolicking. But we survived that, or so I thought anyway.

Towards the end of the 60s we decided we'd like to move back to Cheshire on a more permanent basis. Pat wasn't keen. She was of two minds really. She'd been going back there quite frequently at that time as her mother and sister were there and she seemed to like the idea of being back with the family. On the other hand she enjoyed the different lifestyle of the south east of England: the better weather and other attractions that it has. I felt we could have a higher standard of living in Cheshire, bearing in mind that at this stage I was hardly ever home, having been appointed Managing Director of Sperry Univac, UK and Deputy Chairman towards the end of the 60s. I was out and about pursuing a career with frightening determination. Having been given an opportunity I never imagined I would get, I wanted to make it work and I wanted to make a better standard of living for my family.

So we bought a very nice house in Merseyside, in the Wirral to be precise. This was on the site of a house built for Thomas Henry Ismay who created the White Star Line, where his son Bruce Ismay was living when he experienced the fame and brunt of the loss of the *Titanic*. So it was a house with an aura of history and sombreness about it, and it never actually worked for us at all.

I'm not quite sure when these things started to happen. Travelling at that stage was a key part of my job. All new industries become international quite quickly, and the computer industry did it even faster. Indeed the computer industry was mostly about software rather than hardware. The hardware was simply catching up with the software and was creating the transportation over national boundaries of technology. New technology. New ways of doing things embedded in the software systems that were being moved particularly from the States to Europe. There was also a fair degree of sales support involved, which was the principal part of my job together with some entertaining involving pacifying customers or encouraging people to accept the new products. I was hardly home except at the weekend and then of course I was pretty tired anyway.

I don't think that life could have continued as it was, but hadn't realized just how bad the situation had become until some time in the late seventies when I returned to my office from yet another meeting. My secretary told me that a Mr Bellamy from Warrington had called and would like to speak to me. Normally she wouldn't pass messages on unless she knew I knew the caller and she, like me, assumed it was a Mr Bellamy who was one of our sales representatives in Warrington from the North of England branch. So she got him on the line. It took me a while to work out what was going on. His voice was distinctly different from the Bellamy I knew, and then he came to the point and said he represented my wife and she wanted a divorce. The obvious question I asked him was why she had not discussed this with me. He said she had asked him to handle it for her as her solicitor.

It subsequently came to light during the following thirty years that Bellamy had been a part of my existence. It transpired that my wife had then, and for the ensuing thirty years, been in a long-standing relationship with him. I wasn't quite sure what to make of this situation. However, when I came home that weekend, I was confronted with her and her mother playing a very cagey game, trying to establish a case as to why she wanted to take the matter further. She did not want to discuss the reason for the break-up of the marriage and that was the way it was left. I have to be frank; I was at that stage wondering if there was much point in continuing anyway, with the obvious exception of the children. They were the most difficult part of the situation. I was beginning to wonder what support and what help I was getting out of my matrimonial existence. However, as those of you know who have been divorced, when the solicitor is on board you might as well jump off the ship. Whatever hope there might have been of rescuing the marriage, the moment the law is involved, there is very little chance indeed. I've seen this happen with many couples who have had serious regrets afterwards, but of course there's no turning back when you've got so far. At this time I never really had a satisfactory explanation as to why Pat wanted a divorce although her personal activities became worse as more events came to light. I don't particularly want to dwell on all that stuff – it's so far in the past.

So we were divorced in 1973 and she continued her relationship with Bellamy in its own peculiar form for nearly thirty years until his untimely accidental death in 2001.

It would be unnatural for me to have any other than a critical opinion of the intellectual and even the judgemental abilities of family judges. Their regime of discrimination against men has presided over the last thirty years.

By way of an illustration to make the point the following letter from a lady court usher appeared in one of the major daily papers:

Justice for Men

No man has the ghost of a chance of a successful outcome in an access hearing in court.

He can line the pockets of the legal fraternity, watch the police increase the shine on the seats of their trousers, see legal aid squandered and tissues being made available for all the women who need comforting after their theatrics in the witness box, but he will never get justice.

As a court usher, I've seen many of these women, who are little better than criminals. They neglect their children, have affairs with other men, give their husbands hell, resort to violence and still use every means possible to incriminate their husbands in court.

As far as English law is concerned, 99 per cent of the time simply being a woman means winning the case. The system is overdue for radical change to deal with the bias against men.

The Government must wake up to this cancer spreading in our magistrates' courts and so-called social welfare organisations. Children belong to both parents.

I now face another day in our kangaroo courts, where I'll observe yet more waste in taxpayers' money and police resources, and women dressed up as angels when they've just spent the weekend with their lovers and haven't cared two hoots for their marriage or children.

Name and address supplied to paper but omitted in this extract.

I eventually separated from Pat not in 1973 but twenty-nine years later in 2002, having had many legal battles, paying her two capital sums and with maintenance increasing to reflect my career progress to which she had contributed nothing.

This is partly due to the Bellamy involvement and more particularly a common law judgement in the late 70s which made every application for increased maintenance look at all the financial circumstances anew as if the divorce is current.

There is no logic and little justice in such a judgement and much cost and bitterness paraded in my case over thirty years. There is a strong case for progressive restructuring of this section of the law and how it is administered.

People say about hardworking conscientious people that they put their jobs before their family. But it's not the man's job, it's the family's job. The benefits are going to the family. In fact I've never understood any other arrangement than that of bringing up children in a secure environment. A good wife or a partner is the most valuable asset to have in life, and work is of course only a means to an end to provide security and protection for yourself and your family. Sadly, as we can see from the great many divorces of people in business life, this is a gift which is difficult to find. On balance there seem to be more disrupted marriages.

The French under the guise of social concern enacted legislation making it compulsory that employers ensured their employees worked less than forty hours per week. The sceptics suggested the legislation was designed to share work more widely and thus reduce unemployment and social welfare costs.

The one category of worker exempt from this law was the Executive Manager who, presumably in the interest of the economy and job creation, had to work exceptional hours in the companies' and the country's interest.

This burden is undertaken by executives because there is no choice. It is in the nature of the job that they reason that they are compensated by their wife and family being provided with home and security and in a few cases enjoying a higher standard of living.

A great deal of this endeavour and trust is destroyed by the family courts. If a man takes the affections of a new lady then he naturally must face the financial consequences of continuing to provide for the security and welfare of his family. However it frequently happens his wife, probably not prepared to make the sacrifice of being quite often alone, decides to replace him with another man. Divorce is routine. The battle is over money and on a daily basis regardless of a wife's behaviour, the executive is stripped of his children, his home, his pension in part and his capital and lumbered with debt of on-going maintenance and legal costs for in some cases years to come.

Quite a number never recover the shock of losing so much so quickly when they believed they had committed so much time and effort to the care and concern of their families. When they do they not unreasonably have a scathing opinion of the family law and its non judgmental mechanical mentality. Their difficulty is that few people believe their story because of the secret court system.

A manager's role is to help his people. It is not unusual that a man will want to discuss his matrimonial problems with his boss if he trusts him, so the boss can get some understanding of the difficulties he's faced with, the effect on his work and quite often the effect on his health. Domestic misery is not something you can drop off when you go to work. Work has its own demands and if people are not careful they can find themselves failing both at home and at work and at the ever greater responsibilities imposed upon them by the hostile wife and her lawyers. Too many good men have been destroyed by this arrangement and I do not think the courts have any idea about the effect on people carrying responsibilities. Unless they are the super-rich who can pay and go, or the terribly poor who have nothing to give anyway, it is difficult, and often impossible, for them to contemplate the demands of the legal system and the responsibilities of work at the same time. Kenneth Fleet, that giant of an industrial correspondent, once said, 'The divorce courts are a major power in driving men on.' That no doubt considerably benefits their employer because of the demands their ex-wives impose upon them through the leverage of the courts.

The particular culprits for all this misery are the politicians. They have steadfastly refused to address these social issues and much prefer to put their attention to simpler questions such as giving away public money which makes them feel good and popular and enables them to avoid making serious decisions. If politicians had some guts they would have bitten the bullet and defined some simple rules of divorce which are known to people when they get married.

From my thirty years in the divorce courts I can simply make one simple suggestion. In all divorce it is recognized today that children must come first. It seems we may have gone some distance in defining what is available for welfare for the children in the new Child Support Agency's percentages, which is 10-15 per cent of income or thereabouts for each child up to a maximum of 25 per cent. Unfortunately the Labour politicians damaged the Bill in its progress through the House. They said that it was 10-15 per cent of the husband's income only. This is difficult to understand. It should be 10-15 per cent of both the husband's and the wife's income. The more available for the child the better its welfare. It is chauvinism of the worst form for them to come to such a narrow view in the passage of that Act. If indeed the wife doesn't think she should work but should be at home to look after the children then so be it, then there's no contribution, but if she wants to work then of course she can't provide the home contribution. It's an asinine decision not to take a percentage of both incomes. The capital of both parties should be stated at the outset of marriage and the money available afterwards should be equally divided between both parties, having subtracted the original capital from each of the parties. If there's a house involved, as in some American states the wife should be allowed to live there if she wants until the children grow up. After that the house has to be sold, and the proceeds again equally divided between the parties. There seems no good reason why a man should have to start again all the time, particularly if he gets divorced twice. He is just a soft target for people who want to exploit this weak judicial system that we have in Britain.

Maintenance itself is somewhat difficult, but clearly a wife should be provided for until the children complete full time education or for the same period of the marriage itself, e.g. if ten years, then ten years further support or until the children leave school.

These are quite simple ideas that everyone would understand when they got married. At the moment the only way out of it is that most men simply won't get married and we all know the consequences of that. Short relationships, more single parents, poorer standards of education, crime and no end of things that are rehearsed almost daily in the press, not just in the most popular tabloids but in the more considered broadsheets. Simple rules would avoid much misery. Under the present system people, particularly men, suffer a major reversal in living standard and prospects, and in the case of women, frequently being disgruntled because she hasn't got the lot she thought she had when the divorce took place. This is what she is led to believe by the way the divorce laws are described through the newspapers. She has actually, most times, got the lot, but in her mind she feels there is some more there somewhere. Wives always feel there's a lot more money, and they always feel that future ex-husbands have a lot of affairs; it's a pretty common trait. But the situation has arisen because of the way the courts have approached the financial issues. Some lucky people inherit money, but most men who have aspired to a better standard of living have done it through hard work and a very high proportion of these involved in a 'splitting the loot' type of divorce are managers or executives.

The courts, by and large, haven't the faintest idea of what a manager does. I speak from the experience of being in front of nine judges and I never found one any different from the rest. The life of an executive is very different from most jobs and it's certainly not, as it is conceived from the occasional media comment, work pursued by unscrupulous and difficult people wanting to live the high life. In practice most are conscientious, hard-working people who see the non-financial benefits of the growth of a business, the function of their department or company, an end product they can be proud of in terms of the increasing wealth of the company and the country. The work of an executive has a remarkable mobility upwards in both a social and an international setting. It is socially demanding and internationally knows very few boundaries. The responsibilities and the area of activity expand very quickly and the pace of work accelerates in a way almost like a spinning top flying off the table. I found, by examining my old diaries, that over the last fifteen or twenty years I was involved in about 1000 to 1,500 engagements each year, from speeches, conferences, operational boards, general and public meetings, reviews and overseas business tours to meetings over meals, such as lunch or dinner, or even, believe it or not, occasionally breakfast. All this involved extensive travel overseas, long hours – 8 o'clock in the morning to 10 o'clock at night – and probably travelling with two pilot's cases full of documents, such as outstanding reports and correspondence, which had to be dealt with urgently. It is not unlike the life of a politician who achieves ministerial status. It has constant change of people, places, issues. There is no time to be ill and I can't remember having a day off work in my business life. This kind of living starts very early in the career and it is the person's ability to cope or even endure this regime that determines who is going to make the executive grade.

My father died in 1969. Although he wasn't in continuous contact with the family one of us had generally seen him. But in 1969 we had hardly seen him at all for one reason or another. I think I had lunch with him halfway through the year and that was about it. My mother was concerned that I should set about and go to visit him, but I couldn't get any response when I telephoned. He lived for many years with his great friend and his wife and when I arrived at the house on a bitter snow-swept night towards the end of December the person who answered the door was unrecognizable. It turned out to be his friend's mother who gave me the awful news that both her son and his wife had died quite suddenly and my father was living somewhere else and as far as she knew he wasn't very well either. I then went to find his doctor who was very upset about being disturbed at 7.30 in the evening and informed me, quite callously, that my father was chronically ill and wouldn't last much longer. He told me where he was and I actually found him. I had an extraordinary surprise because although he was very ill indeed, in his own mind he felt he was suffering from flu which he had had for some months. Of course it was far worse than that and he clearly wasn't going to live much longer. He did actually die two days later and I have always been grateful that I found him before events overtook us.

My father's death clearly changed my life. Some time earlier I'd been offered my first general management position. I wasn't too keen as I preferred to be technical director and understand what I was dealing with. For some reason or another the death of my father opened up all sorts of ambitions and doors. By good luck the position was re-offered to me. I took it. That was the beginning of my general management career.

A book called *Future Shock*, written by Tofner was published in the early seventies. Tofner drew an analogy between 'Cultural Shock' and what is described as 'Future Shock' experiences. Cultural shock is when someone is transported at short notice to another country and finds it all too alien and difficult. An example would be a Frenchman who suddenly finds himself in South America, in a Spanish or Portuguese speaking country, surrounded by practices, habits, food and cultural behaviour that he has never experienced before. Tofner described Future Shock as that in the next thirty years coming into the twenty-first century, life would get more and more complicated. People would do more and more things, travel further, experience more, have more and more responsibilities and life would be far more hectic. People would change partners, jobs, towns, friends – indeed the whole mode of life would be about constant change at every level. The difference between Future Shock and Culture Shock is that in Culture Shock you can go back – the Frenchman can go back home to France and carry on his normal life – but with Future Shock there is no way back. A person can opt out, but that's a very lonely difficult experience that is quite alien anyway. He can compromise and try to slow the pace of life down, but that's difficult. He will want to conform to his new high velocity existence and learn to cope with it and the stresses of new society.

This of course is what has happened in modern marriage with people of upward ambition and broad mental dimensions. All these experiences have come on board, which coupled with inadequate judicial arrangements are really the source of all these difficulties but the Courts seem to have no answer to it. The basis for decisions on divorce financial matters broadly speaking stems from the Matrimonial Causes Act 1973 interpreted in a court judgement by Lord Denning in the same year. Denning decided what was good for people's lives or in this case for two people's lives. This was to be the template for everybody else that followed. People arrive at this particular juncture in their lives and someone without the vaguest idea who the people involved are, decides how to split people up for the rest of their lives. For a judge to put people in gaol is one thing and no doubt many people would be good at that but to tell people how to live their lives is the kind of decision few of us would want to make if we knew the consequences of it.

British family law is very much out of line with that of other countries. People should jointly agree arrangements that put them apart totally and completely. The court proceedings are mostly secret apart from a few Appeal Court judgements that become the criteria for other cases. The public don't know what is going on inside the divorce courts. The hearings are held in secret. You don't know the basis of any judgement and when you hear the outcome it is only hearsay, through other people. Parliamentarians elected to define laws reflecting public interest take little interest in divorce law and the public have no influence or knowledge as to what is happening. The courts should be held in public, and the public should have access to them. They would not be interested in most of the cases, but they certainly would be interested in people they knew. They might well go along to understand the basis on which these decisions are being made and once the decision was made it would be tested against public opinion and reaction. The judges themselves would have feedback so that they could start to develop a more realistic approach to the separation of people's lives.

The inadequate behaviour of the Family Division was illustrated in what I hope is the final order in the affairs of my first wife by the direction of the High Court Judge, no less, who had pontificated on consented words in an agreed order to remove the Court's obligated commitment to agree the order to be of little significance. Thirty years of conflict, massive costs and all he was concerned about was to avoid any responsibility. His weapon was that he wanted barristers present to present the arguments. He knew full well the costs involved would let him bully his way to what he wanted: to protect an inadequate system.

His competence was illustrated by his order stating the divorce took place in 1873, two centuries prior. More cost and court time were required to get the century right.

The loss of my mother in September 1985 was a terrible shock for me. I had never known anybody with such profound common sense, such insight, humility and concern. Where she got all these characteristics from I'll never know because she spent her entire life in Liverpool. I can't recall her ever travelling outside the city. Fortunately she was in reasonably good health until the day before she was smitten with a stroke and we were able to have a final conversation. It's a terrible thing, losing a parent, particularly a mother you have such love and affection for.

The ongoing financial disputes with my first wife were rather unfortunate, because I'd married again in 1978. Carol was a woman of many talents and with quite a vivacious personality. A fantastic cook, no question about that. A very good hostess. She was popular with men. Wherever there were men she was busily making conversation with them, but by the same ilk, she was unpopular with women. I never quite work out the psychology of women who dislike other women, but I can see that the way she behaved towards them might lead to a certain amount of social disagreement.

That marriage didn't last very long, from 1978 until 1982, four years during which my two sons were born. I won't bore you with the details of this break-up except in two respects. Firstly, Carol studied assiduously my first wife Pat's behaviour in this whole divorce

Left to right: Robert, Samantha, Desmond, Norma, Stephanie, Nick.
In front, Elena, Sam and Mac.

situation. She copied her techniques to a T. Secondly she was faster to prosecute, but then quicker to agree than her predecessor. She had no pecuniary sense whatsoever. I quickly decided that this would not make for happiness for the rest of my life and against the horrible experience of my first divorce decided that this was going to have to go the same way. So that was brought to a quick end. It cost me the greater part of my capital; that's the price I paid. But it cost me very little commitment to maintaining her, except of course for maintaining the boys, who were still quite young then, for their education through public school. It was not a lot of fun having two of these cases going on at the same time in 1984. In fact at one particular time I was in two different courts on two different cases, tackling this particular problem.

So you see, my personal life has been dominated by my divorce experience. I joke about it. That's the only way to approach it. And I really feel the benefit I got from my children was an indescribable bonus from the whole thing.

I'm really proud of my daughters, who have achieved a wonderful family relationship with their children and both have also been very

Left to right: Andrew, Steph, Dad, Sam, George; 120th birthday party: twins 30, author 60.

George and Andrew at school.

good in their chosen fields. Stephanie is in public relations, running her own company which just about covers every conceivable problem and difficulty, success and failure you can think of for a small business like that. Samantha is a financial services adviser – so swift with the numbers I don't quite know where she picked them all up, but she is certainly good at doing deals in a short period of time. Both of them produced super grandchildren. Steph has got two sons, Sam and Mac and Sam has got a lovely daughter named Elena and a son named Rocco.

Any man that has two sons as well as two daughters is very

privileged indeed. George is twenty-four and Andrew, a couple of years younger. Both show an enthusiasm to get involved and enjoy life. Whatever I have achieved I feel it will be much more difficult for them in contemporary times. However they are going about it the right way, sensing and testing the opportunities before pouncing in and committing themselves to narrow avenues.

Executives can't take their sons into a company to follow them. The boys in their own way and own time will find their niche in life.

In 1991 I was appointed Knight of the Order of St Hubertus, an Austrian chivalry which goes back 600 years devoted to the care and preservation of all animals and birds, based on the argument that mankind has the intelligence and it is our duty to see that there should always be two of every species. It is an interesting institution which was in the province of the Hapsburg family. Of course when they ruled the Austro-Hungarian Empire it was then a Royal privilege and I met some very interesting people from different parts of Europe. I was never involved very much apart from a grand investiture lunch and occasional meetings with some of the nice people years afterwards.

In 1993 I was voted Businessman of the Year for Merseyside and North Wales. Regretfully I was not at the particular ceremony when the announcement was made. The prize was a handsome fruit bowl which I still admire from time to time at home and the prize-giving was in the wonderful St George's Hall, one of Britain's finest buildings, with of course a business dinner. I really felt proud and flattered to be elected to that position and was disappointed in myself for lacking the savvy to make sure I was there. I was in Australia at the time trying to progress some business for North West Water, which was eventually successful and resulted in contracts in Sydney and Melbourne. 1992 brought my Knighthood. I'm not quite sure why I was one of the lucky chosen few. I know lots of other people who were equally, if not more, deserving of such an accolade, but it was possibly for my work at Merseyside Development Corporation or as Littlewoods' most senior employee as the largest commercial employer in Merseyside. The citation read 'for services to the citizens of Liverpool'. It's a very nice thought that I very

Norma.

much appreciate. One thing about receiving an Honour is the large number of letters you get which convey all sorts of hidden feelings towards you that you didn't realize people had. It is also interesting for the omissions from people you would have expected to write. It's a very revealing experience, suddenly being recognized in that way and to watch people's reactions.

Of my great deal of good luck the best was meeting Norma. We both find real happiness in each other's company which makes my setbacks of earlier years of little consequence.

I gave a number of lectures to various public schools on Information Technology and the business of being an executive and they were very well received, because by and large usually the speakers were lawyers and politicians and those older professions. They particularly liked the business idea and my style of lecturing was to talk for about half an hour and then ask for questions for an hour and bring everyone into the conversation. It went well and I know that the students enjoyed them and I enjoyed giving them. A similar thing happened at Manchester University and for one reason or another I ended up as the visiting Professor of Business Policy, which I think was a great privilege.

If you want to be an executive – and so many of them get divorced – I think you have to take into account and decide most carefully, first of all if you do want to get married and be with that person, and what is the basis of the on-going relationship once you get married. This is a decision I don't have to make any more, thank goodness. I've often been questioned by younger people who have seen my particular situation and I've given the only advice you should give to anybody: 'Just do what you think is right for you.' I can simply point out the dangers. It doesn't necessarily mean they'll be overtaken by them. But they themselves will just have to accept that the disasters of modern marriage are very possible for someone who goes into the executive life.

My other interests, which I'm very devoted to, particularly with my present wife, are music and opera. We listen to and attend the opera as frequently as we can as well as going to concerts. I have tried to help to support the various opera authorities and sponsor concerts over a period of time.

Golf, we both play rather inadequately, but that's not the point; we enjoy playing together. In these later years we look forward to more enjoyable holidays, particularly in warm climates.

I know much of this personal aspect has been touching on divorce as that's been a complex issue, but unquestionably since I met my wife Norma seventeen years ago my life changed. You've got to feel when you've had two messy divorces as I have that there might be something wrong with yourself in terms of forming human relationships. As it happens I never had any difficulty in relating to women. Quite the reverse: I've always enjoyed their company very much, so it didn't really seem to be something in that department. But you still question yourself, wondering why it is that you've never been able to sustain a close intimate relationship over a long period of time. Now I understand. However, it takes someone to help you understand the importance of trust, reliability, confidence, honesty and all these other good characteristics in a human being which all of us must have some of. Norma was that person.

Index